TOM HEIMBERG

Making a Musical Life

STRING LETTER PUBLISHING

Publisher: David A. Lusterman
Editor: Mary VanClay
Director of Production and Book Publishing: Ellen Richman
Designers: Trpti Vanessa Todd and Christi Payne
Marketing Manager: Graham Pellettieri
Proofreader: Jessamyn Reeves-Brown

David A. Lusterman, Publisher
ISBN 978-1-890490-59-1

Cover photograph by Jill Nierman,
Courtesy of the Estate of Tom Heimberg.

Printed in the United States of America.
 This book was produced
by String Letter Publishing, Inc.
PO Box 767, San Anselmo, California 94979
(415) 485-6946; www.stringletter.com

Library of Congress Cataloging-in-Publication Data
Heimberg, Tom, 1937-2006.
Making a musical life / Tom Heimberg.
p. cm. -- (Backstage books)
ISBN 978-1-890490-59-1 (pbk.)
1. Music--Instruction and study. 2. Stringed instruments--Instruction and study. 3. Music--Vocational guidance. 4. Heimberg, Tom, 1937-2006. I. Title.

MT170.H45 2007
787.3'092--dc22
[B]

2007001575

CONTENTS

PART III: VIEWS FROM THE MUSICAL LIFE

Foreword

THERE ARE LOTS OF TALENTED MUSICIANS in the world. Tom Heimberg was something more rare: a professional musician, in the best sense of the term. Aspiring musicians, and those music lovers who don't know the intricacies of the profession, would do well to look at the life of my best friend Tom, the model for an accomplished working musician, insightful educator, and generous colleague.

Tom and I grew up together in Hollywood. We played in the Bancroft Junior High School senior orchestra in an era when a public middle school had not one but two orchestras, as well as a band, along with beginning strings and wind classes. There was lots of music in the air and on the air. We took for granted that the NBC Symphony and the New York Philharmonic would broadcast weekly, and our own Los Angeles Philharmonic children's concerts were heard coast to coast.

We met in Mr. Shesler's drafting class for seventh grade boys. It was in the spring of 1949, when we both turned 12. The big red Pacific Electric streetcar took me to school along Santa Monica Boulevard. I was not very happy in the rough world of junior high school. Tom, with his compassionate intuition, immediately introduced himself and offered his friendship, which was to last for a lifetime.

Even at that age, Tom was a philosopher, with a quick wit and a comic talent (we used to do imitations of our eccentric teachers). Our close circle of nerdy intellectual friends included some young professional radio actors of 11 or 12, and that association led to the formation of an after-school drama club. The group gathered often at the home of our friend Arianne, daughter of the distinguished director Edgar Ulmer. This was a circle of very bright kids who were great company. Arianne's father had stories about many great musicians with whom he had worked, most notably as director of the motion picture *Carnegie Hall*. It was a pretty heady atmosphere for a couple of boys from the south side of the tracks.

Our friend Arnold Steinhardt, who went on to be a founding member and the principal violinist of the Guarneri String Quartet, grew up on the same side of the tracks and was concertmaster of our school orchestra. Herb Alpert played trumpet in that orchestra and was student body president. We all learned a great deal from our inspired music teacher, Maurice Ives, who led his adolescent musicians to win top honors at the regional festivals.

Tom adored his violin teacher, Gilbert Back, a member of the Los Angeles Philharmonic who had played in the Berlin Philharmonic in the early '30s. Back was encouraging to Tom, who was a relatively late bloomer but a very conscientious student. In that conscientiousness and intelligence, Back saw the makings of a professional musician. He became a true mentor to Tom, sharing a depth of experience that Tom appreciated.

Tom and I were big music fans. We listened to KFAC, the classical-music station. Tom would call me up at all hours if he heard a piece that excited him, saying, "Linc, quick, turn on K'fack! Francescatti is playing the Tchaikovsky." We played Mozart violin concertos and Schubert sonatinas together and took long, early-morning walks in the Hollywood hills. The talk was about music, girls, and spirituality, as Tom was a very unusual young man for the 1950s: an excellent student, a brilliant chess player, and a disciplined spiritual aspirant who meditated every day. Tom's interest in Eastern religion sprang from his talks with my mother, Nancy Pope Mayorga, who was a Vedantist. He read voraciously on spiritual matters, went to the Vedanta temple in Hollywood, and aspired to a monastic life during his high school and college years. He would observe pretty girls at the swimming pool from the perspective of a chaste monk, commenting to me, "Lincoln, may I call your attention to an excellent manifestation of Holy Mother, over by the diving board!"

Throughout his childhood and teen years, Tom suffered from stomach trouble, which he handled with his characteristic humor. I remember walking home after a swim at the public pool when suddenly Tom assumed the stance of Don Quixote at the windmills. "At the present moment, an ulcer is attacking me," he would say. "Stand aside, ulcer! Get back! *En garde!*" Then he would slip into the market, pick up a quart of milk, down it in about three gulps, and announce, "The enemy has been defeated!"

Tom was always brilliant. Academically he was way ahead of the pack, and as an outstanding graduate student at UCLA, he was encouraged to become an English professor. He was also a very funny man. He could have had a career as a fine actor, or a stand-up comic in the tradition of Sid Caesar. Many years later, I conducted a concert for the real Sid Caesar, and I thought to myself at the time that a comparison might favor Tom. But Tom made a serious, conscious decision: He would become a professional musician.

Tom's strongest attributes as a young music student were musical sensitivity, great industry and patience, and a quick, analytical mind. He came to fruition as a musician at an age when he could fully appreciate the privilege of playing well, working with others, and making a living in music.

In 1961 I was privileged to be best man at the wedding of Rosalyn Metzger and Tom Heimberg. Rosalyn is not only brilliant and beautiful, but a very funny lady in her own right. The newlyweds posed for a series of hilarious wedding pictures, mugging like a vaudeville comedy team. The union gave Tom the opportunity to become the most loving father one can imagine to dynamic daughters Erica and Rebecca, and grandfather to Erica's two boys. The family was put to the ultimate test by the tragic loss of Becky in 1990, which devastated all of us who knew her.

Shortly after they were married, Tom played viola in California in the Oakland Symphony. He then received a Fulbright Scholarship for study in Europe at the Paris Conservatory, and he stayed on in Paris for a second year as an instructor at the Institut Catholique. Then Josef Krips, newly designated conductor of the San Francisco Symphony, held auditions in Vienna. Tom was prepared. He flew to Vienna for the audition, and Krips offered him the position in San Francisco. Tom had to make up his mind between the Minnesota Orchestra, which also wanted him, and San Francisco. No contest! Tom later joked that he had to fly across the Atlantic and back to make the 12-mile jump from Oakland to the San Francisco Opera House.

The period during which Tom served as personnel manager for the Opera Orchestra showed professional strengths other than his playing ability: as diplomatic liaison between management and the orchestra; as a discerning musicians' contractor who hired on the basis of ability, not politics; as an idealistic union man, a fair-minded negotiator who was able to weigh both sides of an issue; and as an orchestra manager of great knowledge, skill, and organization. He handled the orchestral requirements of an opera company that was more complex than Barnum and Bailey, and all with enthusiasm, good grace, humor, and an eye for the bottom line.

Tom Heimberg's professional experience adds up to an overview that is unique. He gives us a glimpse of his philosophy through his many valuable articles about practice technique and other aspects of music and the profession. In an age of synthesizers and solitary, digital-musical emptiness, Tom's life demonstrates that it is the team player who will ensure the survival of true, collaborative music.

I can't think of any personal history so important at this time, and for generations to come, as the working life of Tom Heimberg.

Lincoln Mayorga
Chatham, New York
December 2006

Introduction

TOM HEIMBERG PASSED AWAY on November 14, 2006, and at that profoundly sad moment, I lost a dear friend whom I had known for more than half a century. Tom and I met at age 12 while playing handball during school recess. We performed together in junior high orchestra; played chess occasionally (I poorly); once listened, transfixed, to a nightingale's unforgettable song as we sat in my parents' living room; met in glamorous places like New York and Paris, and in very unglamorous ones that will go unnamed; played Mozart duets for fun; heard each other's concerts; and shared in numerous adventures, along with his wife, Rosalyn, as we journeyed through decade after decade of our lives. A lot can happen in 57 years. But cherished as those memories are, it is Tom's turn of phrase, his smile, the twinkle in his eyes while making a point, and his essential spirit that I want to hold onto and treasure now that he is gone.

Tom's childhood was both blessed with love and afflicted by adversity. His father left home and died when Tom was very young; his mother remarried; and, related or not to those difficult times, he suffered from serious and ongoing health problems during his adolescent years. I suppose that coming to grips with and ultimately surmounting these issues helped forge his essential character, but so did literature, chess, and above all, music—music not only for its alluring strands of sound but also as a secret gateway to things of the spirit. In the first verse of a poem that Tom cherished—one that was written by his father, Thomas Bernard Crotty—I see elements of Tom himself:

> Music, that is God's memory, never forgets you.
> Music, in atom and star, and the falling leaf,
> Binding all worlds in one, remembers forever
> The least light whisper and cry of our joy and grief.

When I went away to music school, Tom rented my room from my parents while he attended college. This afforded us considerable time together when I returned home during school vacations. Tom could be wildly funny—he was in effect a first-class stand-up comic—but he could just as easily move to serious subjects and penetrating thought: "The least light whisper and cry of our joy and grief," as Tom's father put it. Implicit in spending time with Tom was that I too had the freedom to be over-the-edge silly, and the ability to slip into uncharted zones of feeling.

What else do I cherish about Tom? His stories, of course. Tom was always telling stories. Over the years, he must have let me in on dozens of vignettes that he picked up from various sources: from his orchestra stand-partners, his carpool group, a chess opponent, or from singers he had run into backstage before a San Francisco Opera performance. The stories tended to be deceptively modest little items, often humorous; but lurking below their surface were inevitably larger truths. I think that is what Tom loved about them, even needed from them; for aside from the brilliance of his adult life as musician, teacher, writer, chess enthusiast, and orchestra manager, he was at heart a searcher. Tom searched for no less than the meaning of life, wherever and however he might be able to find it.

Some time ago, Tom told me the following anecdote: Serge Koussevitsky, conductor of the Boston Symphony Orchestra, asked Eugene Lehner, the distinguished violist and a member of the orchestra's viola section, to perform Béla Bartók's Viola Concerto in Carnegie Hall. Lehner is supposed to have answered, "Maestro Koussevitsky, each and every one of us has to die sometime, but I would rather not know the exact time and place." This was the kind of story that Tom relished. I don't remember our conversation after Tom delivered, with a raised eyebrow, Lehner's wry observation, but it could easily have led to a discussion about stage fright, which in turn might be the reason his thoughts on the subject appeared some months later in a national music magazine.

Eugene Lehner stated the obvious: Each and every one of us has to die sooner or later. Less obvious is whether some part of who we are will survive among the living to be remembered and valued. For those of us who were privileged to know Tom Heimberg, his humor, his compassion, his playing, and his turn of mind will remain in our hearts and minds for the duration of our own lives. For those who did not know him, Tom has a leg up on most people through his writing. We will never have to say such things as, "Tom? You didn't know Tom Heimberg? What a remarkable man he was. I wish you had known him." The articles included in this book will be of immense practical value to musicians, and they offer a rare insider's view to music lovers who have never been on the other side of the footlights, but they also reveal a great deal about Tom Heimberg, the man that I loved and admired.

One of Tom's articles, "Contract Tips for the Gigging Player," begins with the following:

> Dear Mr. Heifetz,
> Please come to my birthday party.
> (P.S. Please don't forget to bring your violin.)

I was immediately reminded of Heifetz' response when actually asked to play at someone's party. "Would you ask Joe Louis [then reigning heavyweight boxing champion of the world] to box with someone here?"

Tom would have loved that one.

Arnold Steinhardt
New York, New York
December 2006

Preface

I AM GRATEFUL FOR THE LIFE that I have lived. It has been a musical life, a life informed and impelled by the shapes and powers of music. Music has supported me—in all the meanings of that word—for more than half a century.

And what wonderful support that has been. Music is more than sounds in the air. We all learn from music; it is the great symbol of Unity in Diversity, Oneness in Many. Working with the harmonies of music gives us the opportunity to harmonize ourselves, to blend our feelings and thoughts and the ways we move.

As a professional violist, I have been in the classical music world for more than 50 years, playing in the Oakland Symphony, the San Francisco Symphony, and the San Francisco Opera Orchestra. I also worked as the Opera's orchestra manager and managed numerous other orchestras. I have auditioned, hired, taught, mentored, and played alongside hundreds of musicians over the years. As a teacher, I have been devoted to developing practice methods that hone my students' awareness and help them develop the skills to play in the way they intend. For more than 25 years, I have taught a class entitled "The Art of Practice" at the San Francisco Conservatory of Music, which has helped me organize and communicate my views of practice.

Creating a musical life can be a joyful experience, one of working to reach aesthetic ideals. At the same time, devoting our lives to music brings practical and physical challenges—but these can also be gifts when approached with learning in mind. This book sheds light on many aspects of the musical life that we encounter on this journey:

- Methods to attune our bodies and nervous systems, and to align them with our musical goals through practice;
- Thoughts about how teachers and students can share valuable information and awareness, and about styles of teaching and learning that can benefit our playing;
- Valuable tips on performing, enhancing our relationship with the audience, and coping with professional life as musicians; and

- Stories about the many joys of the musical life: playing, working with others, being a part of a musical community, and belonging to musical history.

It has been one of the blessings of my musical life that I have had kind and helpful teachers, and I would like to name and honor them here. Each understood valuable principles about teaching and practice that I develop throughout this book.

The first is Gilbert Back, a violinist formerly with the Berlin Philharmonic who escaped Germany when Hitler came to power. I met him when I was ten years old. I was studying violin casually but wanted to be more serious about it. Through divine grace, my stepfather, who was a waiter at a small delicatessen in Los Angeles, started talking to a customer with a violin case. Thus I became Gilbert Back's first student in America, and he was my teacher for the next 13 years. He taught by showing me how to pay attention to my body—for example, to feel the intervals in my hands before I touched the strings of my violin.

I was also blessed when I was 12 years old to take a summer course focused on radio speaking at the Young Actors Company of Los Angeles, run by master theater teacher Viola Spolin. One of my great memories of this class was that we recorded—onto acetate disks, very high-tech for the times—a funny, short script on the first day of class. We then put the recording away for the summer and continued with vocal exercises for the next two months. On the last day of class, we read and recorded the scripts again, and then compared the two recordings. The contrast was striking. I gained a valuable insight about learning: You don't have to keep the goal always in mind if you're following the right path toward the goal.

Leon Pascal, my teacher when I studied in Paris as a Fulbright Scholar, helped me change a habit of holding up my finger when I played. He wrote out simple exercises for me to play, which I realized had been designed to keep that finger down, so that I learned physically rather than having to think about that finger all the time. It was a wonderful lesson in practice and teaching. He also once told me, when we were talking about teaching, that he never yelled at a student. Playing the instrument was hard enough.

I also want to honor my voice teacher Orva Hoskinson, who enriched my experience as a student through his excitement about the world of opera and the stage. I greatly enjoyed his enthusiasm, and his dramatic and perceptive demonstrations of how I could bring more emotion to my singing voice. He helped me glimpse the experience of opera singers, whom I have so often heard, unseen, from the Opera House orchestra pit.

And, of course, there is the irrepressible Harry Rumpler; read on to Part One of this book for a taste of his inimitable teaching style.

Whether you are a person who is newly developing or renewing your musical practice, an experienced professional, a teacher looking for new inspiration to help guide and encourage your students, or an aficionado of the fascinating stories within musical history, you will find ideas within these pages that will, I hope, help you in your practice and work life, and that will inspire you to find joy in music.

Tom Heimberg, with Erica Heimberg
Kensington, California
October 2006

PART ONE
PRACTICE

I studied with Harry Rumpler, who was always encouraging and positive, yet demanding at the same time. When I was already playing with the Oakland Symphony, I brought a Milhaud piece to a lesson; its rhythms were giving me trouble. As I began to play the piece, Harry started waving his arms and shouting from across the room, "No, no! Stop, stop! Young man, if you do not know what you are trying to do before you try to do it, how will you know, when you have finished trying, whether you've done it or not? Put down that viola and count!"

We need to set our intentions clearly as we begin to practice, and shape each practice session like a work of art. At the same time, we need to let go of our expectation of an immediate result. Cultivate your practice and your musical life like a garden, and let the results arise from within you.

The Mind in Practice 1

It all begins in the brain!

—Luciano Pavarotti, about singing (in private conversation, 1972, in the days when you could get anywhere near him)

PRACTICE IS THE ONLY WAY to learn the viola, or any other human skill. The passion and desire that impel us toward music will energize our practice for a lifetime—but we still have to know what to do. Since we spend tens of thousands of hours of our lives practicing, we do ourselves great good by learning to make our practice more effective, more efficient, more graceful. The better we understand how to practice, the better we will do it. This chapter is a technical exploration of practice.

Practicing is a skill that can be learned and cultivated. Throughout our studies, good teaching brings order and method to our work. Using example, explanation, description, and encouragement, the teacher helps us find our way toward knowing and doing what needs to be done. By following instructions and imitating good examples, we discover how the teacher does this, and we make that ability our own. We learn the craft of practice; we become our own instructors.

The collective teaching experience of the past has bequeathed us a rich legacy of potent practice devices to aid this self-instruction. Modern studies of skill acquisition and body awareness have further deepened our understanding of the conditions in which learning happens, revealing new ways to shape our work. But first we will address an often overlooked truth: Practicing is not mindless repetition. True practicing is done with attention and alertness. So let's start by considering the most important component of any practice session—the mind of the practicer.

One of the deepest and most important mysteries of human existence is the relationship between private mental experience and what we call "the outside world." We know such a relationship exists: When hungry, we can find food. We can make plans that sometimes work. And yet our busy, turbulent thoughts range from dreams to distraction, from obsession to absentmindedness. Fragments of melody, scraps of conversations, memories, dreams, reflections—these make up the hubbub of our minds.

The miracle in all this ferment is that the mind (our consciousness) can sometimes take control of itself—when we remember to let it do so. Out of the rush and welter of our daily concerns, we can direct our minds and use them as fine instruments. We can take charge with purpose.

Two uses of the mind are essential for quality practice: calm self-observation and precise, intentional action. Like themes in a sonata form, these two mental dynamics wind around each other throughout every practice session. Let's look at each of them in turn.

CALM SELF-OBSERVATION

Calm self-observation is the ability to sense and attend to one's own behavior and action with interest and acceptance, and without judgment—like a wise teacher: alert, patient, and kind. The act of observation is not an occasion to praise ourselves when we like what we see, nor to beat up on ourselves when we don't. It is not a reverie about thoughts and feelings, nor an unthinking reaction to stimuli. Calm self-observation is caring attention given to our actions and movements as we make them.

Here is a thought-experiment to perform even as you read this page. You may already be aware of your surroundings—the light you're reading by, fragrances in the air, the sounds around you. Now extend your attention further. While continuing to read, notice the angle of your head, the relaxation or tension of the muscles around your mouth, the lift or hang of your shoulders—feel the depth of your breathing, the lie of your fingers on the page, the posture of your whole body in its balanced interaction with gravity. Attend to those senses that tell you about your body's position in space. Don't try to change anything for now. Don't move or shift or stretch; just observe.

And notice, too, that by this act of observation you have changed your experience of the moment. You have heightened your sense of yourself as a presence. Such moments of self-awareness are precious in themselves. They are also opportunities to be open to learning, and to the changes that learning brings.

PRECISE, INTENTIONAL ACTION

Observation alone is one important use of our minds—making our actions intentional is another. Observation lets us take stock of where we are, but to get something done we must act. By practicing, we build a bridge between our thoughts and our actions. We do this by complementing self-observation with precise, intentional action.

A major goal in practice is to get from one note to another accurately—with the least possible confusion and effort. To ensure this precision, we must anticipate what's coming. When practicing, we do this by creating a conscious pause between deciding on an action and physically doing it. During that pause, we mentally rehearse what we are going to do: We feel the movements before we do them; we hear the sounds before we make them.

After this imaging, we act, and observe ourselves during that action. We observe both the musical task at hand (knowledge of results) and how it feels to do that task (kinesthetic feedback). Then, after acting, we compare and contrast the actual experience with what we imagined. With each successive trial, we try to imagine the action more clearly, and we try to make the details of what we are doing more accurate. Little by little, we bring the mental image and the physical experience closer together.

Here is another thought experiment to do as you continue to read: Imagine that you are raising your right arm into bowing position to play on the C string (for violists). Don't move, just imagine the gesture. Mentally feel the sensations in your shoulder and elbow, feel the weight of your arm, notice your body's change in balance. Now do the action—and observe yourself doing it. Did the image match the motion? Had you remembered the feeling of your chest expanding? Had you anticipated whether your wrist would hold your hand up or let it hang?

Which did you prefer, the plan or the reality? Was the motion more tense than you wanted? Was the image less clear than you'd like? Try again. Let your conceived action and your real action clarify each other. Make your image of the motion clearer; bring your movement closer to the idea.

This four-step sequence—imagine, act, observe, adjust—is the living heart of good practice. It is a slow-motion variant of what happens when we perform music. In performance, we think ahead, we play in the present, we listen behind (to what we just played), and we make adjustments. And all at once! No wonder performing can be confusing—if we let it be. By slowing down to work in clarity, we help ourselves dispel that confusion before it happens. By thinking about our playing during practice, we train ourselves to know what we will need to think about—and not think about—when we perform.

THE COGNITIVE PHASE

According to one psychological schema, the learning of skills occurs in three phases: the cognitive phase, the associative/repetitive phase, and the automatic phase.

This knowledge helps us clarify our planning. We can use these phases as a structure for our work, though we must always remember that in actual practice they do not occur in a steady, progressive sequence. They continually intertwine and double back on themselves.

In the cognitive phase of skill learning, the player develops an idea of the skill to be practiced. The teacher draws up a lesson plan, a player studies a piece away from the instrument, or some musicians (Rostropovich is one example among many) memorize the music before even picking up their instruments.

For those who might not belong to the silent memorizing group, work done during this phase can include many other activities. It is valuable to study audio and video recordings of the piece to be learned, or of other pieces by the same composer. Attending lessons of more advanced players studying the same or similar pieces is also a way for students to get a preview of the work. Anything that starts to get the music into the player's mind—the sound of it, the look of it, the sense of it—helps him decide where to begin.

THE ASSOCIATIVE/REPETITIVE PHASE

In this phase we pick up our instrument (at last!). The guiding rule for this phase of learning is to move slowly, lightly, and carefully, with precise but gentle gestures. Strong exertion makes subtle observation more difficult. There will be time enough to speed things up, to practice performing, to play for other people. Right now, we are training our nonverbal movement centers—and we want to train them right.

Healthful repetition is the beneficial side effect of mindful exploration. Each time we repeat any fragment of music, we can find ways to play it more efficiently, to make it more expressive and more accurate. Thus repetition and renewal refresh and revitalize one another. Our preparations have shown us what to work on and how to work on it. Now we make connections with what we already know, and build the music into our very being.

There are ways to keep this sequence varied and engaging. Every book dealing with technique offers page after page of possible variations to practice; we should all be accustomed to changing (intentionally) the rhythms or bowings of demanding passages.

We can also add physical variations: After playing a passage several times with normal posture, play it standing on the left foot—a good test of how arm motions affect balance. Since our movements often occur in blocks guided by the eyes and the dynamics of the head-to-neck relationship, we will learn something by altering those blocks. And certainly the passage should be played with eyes closed, as a test of memory.

Contract the moving muscles as little as possible; relax the others as much as possible. Always seek to release unnecessary tension. Remember that mistakes and accidents are our friends when they happen during practice. They show us what to work on. They help us focus our attention. We need to welcome them hospitably, not angrily.

THE AUTOMATIC PHASE

This is the phase in which patterns and movements have become so familiar and so ingrained that we can do them without thinking about them. This doesn't mean we should stop thinking! We can continue to build our abilities into ever-larger units.

Through years of careful practice, every efficient and graceful motion adds to our repertoire of actions and our ability to play without thinking about playing. We develop an inner template of playing, to which we can always add more: technical patterns, musical pieces, increased understanding.

The ability to summon up our interest and sustain our attention is what keeps us loyal to our work. It is how we stay vital and engaged. The simplest change of routine can often bring a practice session to life: Those who are accustomed to practicing seated should stand up. Those who stand should sit. Those who always start scales climbing up from the lowest note should start at the highest note and descend.

IN PRAISE OF PRACTICE

I think of practice as a series of opportunities for success. Opening the door to the practice room is a success. Opening the instrument case (often the hardest part) is a success. Tuning is a success. Getting from one note to the next is a success.

These small successes encourage our practice and nourish our learning. And it is wonderful to have a practice in one's life. Practice connects the days and gives them a core of enduring meaning. Musical practice is a lifelong activity that trains the mind, the body, the expression of musical emotions, and even one's sense of self.

Please take this quick overview as an introduction, and as an invitation to go further. Practice is an activity in which each of us can find our own ways and carve our own personal understandings. All sincere efforts have value, so go forward, and gather deep gratifications.

2 Practice and Self-Observation

AN ANONYMOUS TEACHING MAXIM holds, "The teacher cannot teach what he knows; he can only show how he learned what he knows." Practice is how musicians learn what we know. We spend thousands of hours of our lives doing it. Practice is the way skills are grown, developed, and maintained. And practice itself is a skill that can be learned and cultivated.

Practice sessions are periods of self-training in which you are both teacher and learner, observer and observed. During those periods, you can develop habits that will free you for fuller musical expression.

Notice, also, that simply by observing yourself during these sessions, you change your experience of the moment. You heighten your sense of yourself as a presence. This recognition is a foundation on which any practice can develop.

The famous five senses all inform the brain about the external world. You also have a large array of senses that inform you about your internal world. Of these, the ones that let you know about your body's balance, its movement through space, and the relations of your limbs to your trunk are especially relevant to musical work.

The physical aspect of music practice is training the spatial coordination of senses and movements. You do this by observing both the outside task and the inner experience of doing it. Observing yourself enables you to learn more effectively.

I remember an episode in which calm self-tutoring did not prevail: I was ten years old, working from the J. Hřimaly scale book (*Scale Studies for the Violin*). I was standing up while I played, and I was sagging. The room was hot. The violin felt heavy, and the notes kept coming out wrong. So did I first make myself more comfortable, then analyze the problem and set about solving it in manageable segments? No. I stamped my foot, yelled, and hit the music with my bow, gashing several pages and knocking over the music stand.

I think that I have remembered this incident for more than half a century because immediately afterward I did observe myself—a sudden self-remembering. I had had an outburst and nothing had been accomplished. I just had to pick up and start over again. And now the music was torn. I've never hit music again (even though I've sometimes felt like it).

By contrast, a story from the career of Kay Stern, concertmaster of the San Francisco Opera Orchestra, provides a tribute to the power of objectivity and clear thinking. Some years ago, Kay was looking for a position on the West Coast at a time when there were no violin openings. But San Francisco Opera had announced auditions for a titled viola chair, and she decided to try for it. She rented a viola, was given a beginner's guide to viola notation by a friend ("It was a joke gift, but believe me, I used it"), and started to practice.

"One of the reasons I had a successful viola audition was that I had no history on the instrument, of failure or success," she explains. "If I missed a shift while practicing, I would think, 'That's interesting. There's something I don't know about this shift.' If that had happened on the violin, I might have started to beat up on myself—'Kay! How can you miss that?!'"

I was the union steward for those auditions, and I can attest to the artistic results of her work. The beauty of her playing made listeners sit up and take notice. Yes, she won the position handily.

Moving from violin to viola and back again can be done fairly quickly because the instruments are played in similar ways. Similar, but not identical; Stern's accomplishment is remarkable because she did not let her violin and viola patterns get in each other's way. Players of the violin and viola, through years of attention, practice, and habituation, have developed a repertoire of movement patterns, an inner template of their playing, that they can apply to any similar instrument. This template is the result of sensory-motor training, in which they learn to sense, feel, and understand their body movements.

"Repetition is the mother of learning," says the Russian proverb. But repetition of error and inefficiency will never lead to success. The purpose of practicing is to build abilities, not to repeat what doesn't work. And there is not just one correct way to learn string playing—or any high art—as if it had to be scratched into granite. Hard practice can mean hard muscles, hardheadedness—and in the end, hard playing.

An important aspect of practice is finding ways to replace tension with attention. Tension and stress have been shown to reduce the ability to distinguish subtle sensory differences. Instead, learn by playing slowly, lightly, and softly. Doing so will give you the time to observe and develop understanding. Speed and volume of sound will come after clarity and efficiency have been established.

Practice is a blend of trial and observation. It is important to create a pause between deciding on an action and doing it. Before each action, mentally rehearse what you are going to do. During each action, observe what you are doing.

The mental rehearsal can have many dimensions. You can focus on the movement of a single joint, or you can try to feel the whole choreography of your movements. You can identify the musical materials you are working with—the notes, the intervals, the shape of the phrase, the rhythm. You can decide on the speed and duration of the experiment. Through these mental preparations, you can coordinate your appraisal of the external world with your inner physical sensations. The clearer your perceptions, the clearer that coordination will be. Good craftspeople measure several times before cutting. You can certainly afford to imagine several times before moving.

Sometimes players (younger and older) practice with desperate intensity because they feel overwhelmed by what they are trying to do. Technique seems infinite, repertoire enormous. They start to feel they are running out of time even before they start. At moments like that, the observant pause between thought and action is especially important. Remember that an immense number of technical forms can be reduced to a collection of basic elements and formulas (scales, arpeggios, bowing patterns). When the fundamental elements have been learned mindfully, you can shape them to the specific demands of particular pieces of music.

Observations are improved if you try to see and hear yourself from every possible angle. They are even more pertinent if you scan and identify your internal sensations at the same time. You will advance your understanding further still when you coordinate how you look or sound externally with how you sense yourself. A tape recorder can help you hear yourself objectively, and a metronome offers a trustworthy steadiness of tempo. And if you record yourself along with the metronome, you will clearly hear any discrepancies. A camcorder provides an even better opportunity to watch and hear yourself.

But a full-length mirror can be one of your most important aids. It is instant replay at the speed of light. It allows you to see what you are doing and sense what you are doing, simultaneously. This can lead to quick insights: Even if the notes sound accurate, you will see sudden lunges of position change, awkward string crossings, signs of inappropriate effort.

You can even practice effectively with a mirror while using no instrument at all—air violin! Practice the right- and left-hand movements as shapes in the air. You can monitor them for grace and efficiency, without being distracted—for now—by valid concerns about accuracy and precision.

Another way to practice without the instrument is through mental imaging. Robert Gerle tells us in his excellent book ***The Art of Practicing the Violin*** (Galaxy Music Corp.) how he mentally practiced his repertoire and even learned new pieces while huddled under his bedclothes in a cold Parisian room. Practicing mentally is not a mystic leap into the unknown, but a refinement of what you should do when your instrument is in hand: Think before acting.

Practicing in the ways I have suggested is satisfying and effective. It is also part of a larger project of discovery and insight. Through our observations we not only develop our craft, we develop our picture of the world, and our sense of where we are in that picture.

3 Using Imaging in Practice

MUSICIANS SOMETIMES SAY they practice by reading over parts and scores and then "imagining" what to do. I find that many students are mystified by this idea. What does it really mean? How does imagining something help you play better?

At every level of musicianship, from beginner to expert, we have to think about what we're going to do before we do it. We have to know what we are going to try before we try it.

There are accomplished musicians of long training and high ability who can memorize a piece from the score before they take up their instruments and apply their well-developed technique to it. At the other end of the spectrum are beginners who must slowly work out what the notes are before they start working out how to play them. The rest of us are in between—we all have to think and preplan our work.

That's what I mean when I tell my students (and myself) to "practice smarter, not harder." By "smart," I mean using the distinctively human ability to make a pause between the thinking of an action and the doing of that action. The possibility of that pause—that little space between thought and action—is the basis for awareness. And awareness is the region of our minds that both learns and guides our learning.

Many students are dominated by ideas that are built into our language and our culture: If they "work hard" or "practice hard" or "try and try again," they will improve. They get trapped by the notion that sincerity of effort is shown by severity of effort. They get tense, and they do things tensely—over and over again.

But we do not learn string playing (or any high skill) as if there were just one way to do it. Instead, we grow in our understanding. We try out many ways to play, many subtly different possibilities of movement. We compare how they feel and how they work. As we coordinate movement and hearing and thinking, we develop a repertoire of techniques and actions, and we learn to guide ourselves in selecting the actions that are right for what we want to do.

Attention—self-observation—is required for this work. We develop by attending not only to the goal, but also to ourselves in relation to that goal—and to the means we use to reach that goal. As we persevere in this gentle effort, we find that subtle differences in efficiency and precision can be best felt when the muscles are free of unnecessary tensions and the mind is alert.

Cultivating that all-important alertness is what I call "practicing smarter." And a key means to that end is to imagine each action before doing it. This can be done at any time—while practicing, while reading a score on the bus, while taking a walk.

Here's an example from my teaching: A student of mine flubbed a "finger-twister" several times at a lesson and couldn't figure out why. The reason was close at hand. Though the pattern was within her abilities, it was not yet clear in her thoughts.

The first step toward helping her was to slow her down (less impatient effort, more attention). The second step was to help her clarify the pattern to herself. To do this, I combined several practices. I asked her to play the passage slowly three times, with several added assignments. Before each repetition, she was first to look at the music, then to imagine the sensations of playing it slowly. With each visualized play-through, she was to notice and name aloud a different aspect of the music: First, she named the notes while imaging (then played slowly); second, she named the intervals while imaging (then played slowly again); and finally, she named the fingerings (and played slowly once more). Only after doing all this was she to try the passage up to tempo.

That final a tempo went perfectly. Each previous repetition (there had been six: three imaged and verbalized, three played) clarified the task from a different point of view. In just a few minutes, the pattern had become clear to her. Of course, more practice was needed before that pattern, and the piece it was part of, could be played habitually and dependably. But now she would approach her practice with confidence, knowing that she had already successfully played the difficult spot.

This is just a single example from the large field of mental practice, but it illustrates some specific ways to study music, with or without your instrument in hand. The more clearly you can see, hear, name, and imagine the actions of playing, the better prepared you will be to observe yourself and your work when you actually play.

The goal of string teachers and students should be to set pupils free by helping them become their own teachers. The awareness and self-observation necessary for this freedom begin their growth in the space between thought and action.

4 Self-Teaching Books and Instruction

AFTER 35 YEARS AS A PROFESSIONAL (and 20 years of study before that), I love my viola more than ever. Just as I think that anyone who wants to study music should be able to, I also think that anyone who wants to study the viola should be able to. It can be a lifetime companion.

So what do you do if your career or family life require you to move frequently, and you have trouble staying with one teacher? Students (not my own) sometimes ask me this question, and it poses a dilemma. Despite my belief that study should be possible for anyone, I am reluctant to encourage these students to try to learn solo, without a teacher. I feel like a physician asked to prescribe a cure for a patient he's never met. So my first and strongest suggestion is always that any student find some way to spend time with an experienced, patient teacher who can help plan a program. Even if you can't see your teacher often, a guide who has met you in person—who knows your physical makeup and where you are starting from—will be better able to customize a study plan to your needs. Even written correspondence, exchanging videotapes through the mail, talking over lessons on the phone, or setting up audiovisual phone connections are better than nothing.

If it is absolutely not possible to hook up with a real, live teacher, students will need a program that can provide more than musical directions. They will need to hear examples of correct playing, to see examples of good players. And they will need to be able to see and hear themselves from every possible angle. I recommend all the nonhuman assistance available: A tape recorder helps us hear ourselves more objectively. A metronome offers a steadiness of tempo that is more trustworthy than a tapped foot (or a head beaten against the wall). A full-length mirror helps us monitor our actions while we are doing them. A videorecorder offers a chance to watch and hear "from the outside," like a member of an audience. All of these tools for self-observation can help us to become our own teachers.

So will *The Viola: Complete Guide for Teachers and Students,* by Henry Barrett (University of Alabama Press). This book is packed with guidance and information. In addition to a grading of study books, lists of repertoire, and sample programs, it offers many useful pieces of advice regarding practice. This second edition (1996) also has brief descriptions of several systems of mind and body training (the Feldenkrais Method, the Alexander Technique, and others). Each of these systems works toward self-learning along a different line of approach, and each has relevance to viola playing—as well as to all other aspects of one's life.

Two systematic approaches to string playing, with proven histories, offer good roadmaps to the string-learning territory. *Young Strings in Action* (Boosey and Hawkes) follows the principles and practices developed by Paul Rolland and given shape by him and the Illinois String Research Project more than a quarter of a century ago. Shinichi Suzuki's *Suzuki Violin School* (Summy-Birchard, in several volumes over several years) is famous and familiar. As a beginner's approach, and as a long-term plan with important repertoire presented in sequence, it is very valuable. These two systems can be used together. What makes them especially useful for a solo learner is the amount of backup material available from a variety of sources: In addition to the books of music, there are recordings of the pieces, recordings of accompaniments, and videotapes of students and teachers playing the pieces. There are also teachers' manuals, which you will need in order to act as your own teacher.

The Teaching of Action in String Playing, by Paul Rolland with Marla Mutschler and Frances A. Hellebrandt (Illinois String Research Associates, available through the American String Teachers Association), is a fine book. It has wonderful analytic descriptions of several approaches to string playing as well as specific directions for teaching efficient action in playing. The philosophy is knowing and solid, the directions are clear, the pictures are helpful. It's a good book by a great teacher.

The Suzuki Violinist, by William Starr (Summy-Birchard), is more than a teacher's manual for the Suzuki approach to string playing. It is the advice and reflection of a kind and patient teacher whose long experience with this system richly qualifies him as a guide to its use. Starr describes and endorses past practice and then goes on to expand some of the parameters of the teaching.

Any of these approaches to string playing will offer good guidance, and the library of further material is enormous. There is a whole international culture of string history and knowledge available in books, music, and methods. Like the Hindu saying about chess, it is an ocean from which a gnat may drink, or in which an elephant may swim.

If I list too many books, you won't know whether to drink or swim (there's another job of the live teacher: adjusting the doses of the rich available material to the needs of the pupil). So I will just list a few more old favorites.

Elizabeth A.H. Green has done wonderful work in several areas of music pedagogy. Her contributions to the creation of ***Principles of Violin Playing and Teaching*** by Ivan Galamian (Shar Products Co.) would have been enough in itself. But there is also ***Teaching Stringed Instruments in Classes*** (American String Teachers Association), a sweet summary of principles aimed specifically at class teaching in a progressive sequence. As a solo learner, you will be your own group—teacher, student, observer, and audience—so a book about group teaching is right on track. (This is another valuable publication offered by the American String Teachers Association, or ASTA, at www.astaweb.com; also take a look at the organization's ***American String Teacher*** magazine.)

Also important is the American Viola Society, which offers membership and a variety of services, including the ***Journal of the American Viola Society*** (see www.americanviolasociety.org). The ***Journal*** published a two-part selected bibliography on viola pedagogy by Claudine Pinnell Bigelow in issues 1, 2, and 3 of Volume 9, in 1993. Bigelow's list gives a taste of how large this field really is.

If you ever have a chance to buy a copy of ***The Dounis Principles of Violin Playing,*** by Valborg Leland, grab it! This was a 1949 ***Strad*** magazine publication (reissued in 1963) of enormous practical use. The directions are clear and specific, the images are evocative and helpful. It is a book from which you can learn over and over again; the only thing wrong with it is that it seems to be out of print.

An excellent example of progressive work for graded levels of students is ***Viola Scales and Arpeggios,*** by Marguerite Wilkinson, published by the Associated Board of the Royal Schools of Music.

I am particularly fond of the Harvey Whistler books, published by the Rubank Educational Library and Hal Leonard, and still deservedly in print after all these years; I used them in the early 1960s when I was switching from violin to viola. ***Introducing the Positions for Viola*** comes in several volumes.

Finally, ***String Power—I: Viola,*** by Sally O'Reilly (Neil A. Kjos Music Co.) is a slender volume but a very good introductory primer for viola learners.

I want to offer a few additional words of advice: Remember always that learning the viola is a training of your mind. Whatever text or method you finally choose, the book will tell you what to do, but it will not tell you how to do it, or what state of mind to hold while you do it. The key to good practice is an attitude of interested, generous, and objective self-observation. (***The Inner Game of Music,*** by Barry Green with W. Timothy Gallwey, published by Doubleday, has many excellent exercises to help you stay observant and objective about your work.)

I have often thought that good practice is similar to good gardening. The gardener does not cause the seeds to sprout. But the gardener can help establish good conditions for growth and can maintain those conditions through time. That's like the patience of slow, attentive practice. A good gardener doesn't pull up the plants to see how their roots are doing. A good practicer doesn't speed up too early just to see if he's getting closer to the fast tempo.

Work slowly, lightly, patiently, attentively, and trust the elemental force of learning to sprout and grow.

5 To Preserve, Protect, and Defend Practice Time

THE ART OF MUSIC IS IMPORTANT in every human culture. And there is another great art that makes music possible: the art of practice. Every minute of music ever performed has been preceded by hundreds and thousands of hours of practice time.

Those hours are precious. Art is long, life is busy, and practice time needs to be carved by hand from the rush and tumble of experience. But time so carved can be more than the means to a musical goal—it can be a haven from the sandstorm of details that we call the demands of daily life. It can be an oasis of refreshment and self-affirmation.

Young beginners and students usually don't know this, because adults do their planning for them. For most early learners, practicing is just another thing to do, required and directed by teachers and parents. It's not often their first choice of how to spend time. They want to hang out with their friends. They want to poke at their video games. They want to play—we all do.

But as we grow older, the values and pleasures of dedicated practice become clearer to us, even as the demands of life become more insistent. Our days are full of things that must get done, classes or jobs that must be prepared for, family joys and responsibilities that need attention. In the midst of all this, we must learn to designate and protect our practice time.

Practicing does not happen by itself, at any level. Every aspect of practice requires intention. That is one of its great psychological rewards. When we set a time to practice and keep to it, we have kept an appointment with ourselves. We have made an ongoing connection with the person we are through time. That is a precious benefit of practicing.

Another benefit is that it helps your playing.

The first step toward protecting practice is choosing the right place to do it. If your household has a designated music room, great! If you have access to practice rooms in the school next door, use them. I know many professionals who come early to the hall before a performance, or stay late afterward, to practice.

But resources like those are not always available on a day-to-day basis. If you have to set up a home practice space wherever and whenever you can, seek a privacy that can be protected. Bedrooms, for example, can be excellent practice rooms during the day, provided no one in your family wants to take a nap or do private yoga practice. Bedroom doors are closable, bedrooms are not heavily traveled routes, and a bed is a great place to put an open violin or viola case or to spread music. (But beware of the joking command, "If you're tired, lie down and practice." It does not always work.) Garages can serve at almost any hour. They are handy, though not often cheerful or uplifting.

Once you have determined the space and time of your practice, defend them as diligently as any artist defends studio time. Do you think that people in your household might interrupt you? Take preventive measures. Put a note on the door: "Please do not disturb. I'll be practicing until 6:30—see you then." That usually works for adults (though if your potential interrupters are young children, you might need additional help).

Use an answering machine or a message service on your phone. If a television program that you want to see is scheduled to come on during your practice period, set the machine to record.

Those are some of the ways to take care of intrusive distractions. It is also important to be prepared for the distractions that come from within. Warming up is usually fun; so is playing music you already know. But as soon as you start on something new and difficult, you will get hungry. You can save yourself the interruption of a trip to the refrigerator by having some snacks handy, nibbles that are not gooey or sticky. Have a glass of water or juice close by (but not so close that it could get knocked over or splashed on your instrument).

You are a responsible person, and during a practice session you will think of many responsible things to do: phone calls to make, checks to fill out, letters to write—worthwhile activities whose importance you remember just when they are a distraction from practicing. Be ready for them. Have a notepad and pencil nearby. Jot down what you think of and promise yourself to do it all later, after you've practiced.

With experience you will come to know your own personal susceptibilities to distraction. That knowledge helps you get ready to deal with them ahead of time. Do you tend to stop practicing to trim your nails? Check your nails before you open your case. Do you get tired of sitting, or tired from standing? Get a high stool on which you can perch without breaking the rhythm of your work. I know musicians who say that having a TV set on in the same room helps them get started, while others report that turning on the set for a five-minute break can turn into hours of movie watching. It would be valuable to know to which group you belong.

It's also good to know what your best times are. Students are often advised to do their practicing in the morning, when they're rested and fresh. Morning also lets you get all or part of your practicing done first thing in the day, which is a big plus. But in many households, morning begins more like an exploding hand grenade than a calm awakening. A clarinetist friend of mine says that sometimes he feels that he wakes up 45 minutes behind schedule, no matter what time the alarm rings. His practicing is taken from other parts of the day.

These guidelines are not about perfect conditions. They are about the struggle to make practice time in a world that usually does not care whether we practice or not. Musicians make their practice time out of what is available. For example, Rufus Olivier, the great principal bassoonist of the San Francisco Opera and Ballet Orchestras, once crafted his practicing exactly to his needs. He was preparing an audition and all his solos and excerpts had reached the point where they worked well in the privacy of his studio. But he wanted to be sure he could play them as well in the presence of other people.

So for two weeks he went to a local park every afternoon and practiced. If people stopped to listen, he played his audition for them. If they didn't stop, he still practiced, knowing they were near. By the time the audition came around, he was ready. (Yes, he won.)

This story is inspiring because it shows practice designed for a specific purpose, making use of unconventional resources. It also shows that there is still at least one neighborhood left in America where one can practice bassoon in a public park, safely.

The distinguished trumpeter Marv Nelson, a retired professor of music from California State University, Hayward, admits that he used to practice while driving his car. "Sometimes people in cars next to me would roll down their windows, and I'd play a solo for them. I never got a ticket, and I always watched the road carefully. It was good practice when no other time was available, but I don't think I should recommend it to anyone." Certainly not to string players! But the story does show how far people sometimes go to get that practicing done.

Don Ehrlich, a well-known violist in the San Francisco Symphony, has his own memory of a rare and semipublic work location—a cargo truck. It was at a summer music camp in the state of Washington some years ago. The quartet he belonged to was coaching there for the summer, but faculty practice facilities were not provided. "There was this big truck on the grounds," he explains, "with an enclosed cargo area. I think it was still used to transport things, but mostly it just sat there. It had a small light inside, and if you opened the back door you got more light. I did a lot of practicing in that truck that summer."

My own experience with "automotive practicing" lasted for 17 years. From 1971 to 1988 I owned and ran (at ever-increasing expense) a small, four-cylinder English motor home. I loved that van. It was a Commer van with a Bluebird Highwayman camper shell, and it had enough headroom and space that I could practice without poking anything with my bow—provided I sat at just the right angle on the edge of the bench.

It was great to be able to park on a side street, draw the curtains, and practice for 30 or 40 minutes in the midst of a busy day. Modern automobile ads on television do not impress me. I have owned the car of my dreams, and it had nothing to do with style and road handling.

Arnold Steinhardt, the much-traveled first violinist of the Guarneri String Quartet, has many stories of practice time wrested from a busy schedule on the road. He finds his heavy practice mute invaluable when coping with hotel rooms and jetlag. "Once in the Swiss Alps, in a train compartment at two in the morning, I used the mute and played very softly," he says. "I got in a good half hour of practice before a polite knock on the wall informed me that the sound was still carrying."

Whether riding a rolling train or facing the hassles of daily life, it is up to each of us to make or find our own practice time. Our success will be an outgrowth of our devotion and determination. But it is important to remember that once the time has been staked out, there is a whole world of inner practice skills to learn and use. Setting up the time is just the very important beginning of the art of practice.

6 Personal Practice Planning

GOOD PRACTICING STARTS with good planning. Whether you are squeezing five minutes of practice into a busy day or setting aside an entire afternoon, guidelines can help you sort through the thousands of details that music study and instrument playing entail. There will certainly be adventures in the course of the work: surprises to deal with, experiments to try, problems to solve. But you can be prepared for them if you have a plan to help mobilize your attention and focus your concentration.

When I speak of a plan, I do not mean a lockstep sequence of action. Instead of presetting rigid lines of action, seek out the natural patterns that can inform your endeavors. For example, when performing music, think ahead, play in the present, and listen behind. The same goes for practice—though on a different time scale: plan the future, work toward it now, and then look over what's been accomplished.

From that point of view, simply knowing what you're going to work on is a plan. Whether it is set up just before starting or adopted from a program developed long ago, a plan will give shape to your actions. Know what you're going to do before you begin, and afterward you'll be able to gauge how well you've done it.

Planning starts in the mind, but it need not stay there. A written record of intentions and outcomes—of what succeeded and what didn't—can be a precious source of insight and self-guidance.

Experienced teachers and players have used these ideas throughout history. The literature of music pedagogy is packed with written teaching aids: checklists of repertoire, progressive learning plans, outlines of practice sessions, assignment calendars. You can benefit from these advance labors, rather than reinventing them.

Hal Lepoff, a busy Northern California freelance violinist and teacher, has an interesting approach to his teaching materials. He uses charts with create-a-constellation stars to, as he says, "try to put some organization into my students' practice. For myself, however, I've only ever used blank paper, usually in the form of a journal. Recently when

I had many pieces to prepare, I kept a sort of checklist just to be sure I made the rounds on a regular basis." Blank paper is indeed the universal, all-purpose form.

Barry Green, author of the enduringly useful book ***The Inner Game of Music*** (Doubleday), has developed a pocket-sized lesson journal for his students. In one compact notebook, there are places for listing the student's long-, medium-, and short-term goals, plans for work, and *Inner Game*–oriented questions about the pieces being prepared.

The late Elizabeth Mills, that dedicated and industrious teacher who contributed so much to the Suzuki organization in Southern California and nationally, may be known to some readers as an editor of, and contributor to, ***In the Suzuki Style*** and ***The Suzuki Concept*** (both by Diablo Press), two influential books that are still part of the canon of Suzuki teaching.

Years ago, Mills gave me some notebook materials that she used in her teaching. Called "Fruitful Music Study," the pages are extremely thorough, with special allocations for the familiar items: goals, assignments, practice records, repertoire lists, records of performances given. But the whole package is given a warmth and living unity by her use throughout of the organic metaphor of growing a fruit tree. This image is traced in detail, from the preparation of the soil (listening) and planting of the seed (beginning to practice) through many stages of sprouting, ripening, pruning, and shaping to the bearing of fruit (performance). This beneficent, organic image does much to help develop the patient diligence so important to effective and rewarding practice.

If you feel intimidated by the idea of putting together your own practice planner and would welcome help in getting organized, I can recommend three published planners currently on the market. They are good examples of thoughtful, well-conceived practice tools. All three are sturdy 8½-by-11-inch notebooks, and they share some thematic features, especially calendar templates of one kind or another. But each has its own approach; there is no One Great Big Plan that suits everyone.

The Musician's Practice Planner, published in 1999 by MoltoMusic Publishing (www.moltomusicbooks.com) and already into its second printing, was developed by violist Stephanie Railsback and her husband David Motto, an electric bassist. Based on their combined experience as players and teachers, the *Planner* is efficiently designed for the important task of keeping track of assignments and practice progress. The format is direct and useful: There are double pages for 40 weekly assignment entries (two school semesters) and a practice log, with three extra pages for musical or written notes. The left-hand page—the Weekly Lesson Plan—is for the teacher's use. It has an eight-section grid, plus additional notation room at the bottom. The grid provides spaces for assigning scales, warm-ups, études, exercises, repertoire, and other categories, with additional spaces for listing specific goals. On the facing page—the Daily Practice Log—there are entry areas for the student to log daily practice priorities, metronome markings, time spent on each assignment, and total time for the day.

Clearly the emphasis of this planner is on managing time by making assignments, noting priorities, and keeping track of practice—good purposes all. Railsback says that several teachers she knows are using the book successfully, adding, "It can be livened up with colored pencils and stars for the little kids. Adults can be more serious and use dark pencil or ink."

No fair! I want colored pencils and stars, too. Practicing may be a serious matter, but it needn't be grim; fun helps learning.

If you are seeking something broader than an intensive emphasis on time use, try *The Musicians' Practice Log,* which delves into the very psychology of the practicer. Author Burton Kaplan is well known for his Magic Mountain Marathon Practice Retreats and his seminars on practicing, which have devoted followers all over the country. This log (available from Perception Development Techniques at www.magicmountain music.org) is one of the tools he uses in his teaching of practice.

In addition to the allocation of time (the reusable Practice Time Management Sheet is quite handy), this book attends to the practicer's emotional relationship to the practice experience. Moods, interruptions, ideas, and feelings in the course of practice, and the sense of progress or lack thereof, are important in the complete picture; the book provides a systematic approach to recording and graphing these themes.

The first 15 pages of the book give clear directions on how to use the system. This is followed by 16 weeks' worth of Daily Practice Logs and weekly summaries, followed by sections devoted to weekly and monthly reflections and graphs, technique and repertoire achievement lists, and a performance record.

"During the eight years that I was teaching practice at the Manhattan School," says Kaplan, "I would make this agreement with my students: If they filled out the practice log, they would get an A on that part of the course. Content was never graded; they just had to make entries. It doesn't take very much time—just do it, and at the end of just a month the student might have provided himself with very valuable counsel."

The Musicians' Practice Log is part of a well-thought-out system, and anyone can benefit from using it. In this short description, the amount of record-keeping required might sound formidable, but it's not. It can be done little by little, and it all works toward a better understanding of one's own relationship to practice. That's what counts.

The Practice Handbook: A Musician's Guide to Positive Results in the Practice Room, by Linda M. Gilbert (Damore Publishers), is a very interesting work that accents an awareness of the components of practice. It begins with a short essay, "The Basic Elements of Practice," that deftly touches on such important subjects as body and posture, breathing (aimed at wind players, but string players—who also breathe—can benefit too), physical care, focusing and concentration, goals, and what you can do to learn how to practice.

The Handbook emphasizes two major themes. The first is that practicing is a skill that can be learned and developed, which I endorse with all my heart. The second is that everything in the book is meant to be adapted to individual teacher-student relationships. The included Daily Practice Organizer includes a 25-point checklist of specifics requiring attention (including articulations, bow speed, dynamics, and intonation), a list the practicer is encouraged to expand.

This has been only a brief sampling of some of the written planners musicians use to bring order and focus to their practice. Because of their range of approaches, I encourage practicers to seek out all three of these books, as well as others.

And there are many other methods. The literature offers a variety of useful ideas and promptings, and anything that helps is fine. There are as many needs to be satisfied as there are practicers.

This kind of research can go deep, but it is important to remember that any organizer is a tool, not a task. All are aids to the loving persistence that keeps practice moving and that best serves music and musicians.

7 Building a Personal Practice Book

MUSIC IS LONG, and practice time is precious. Finding efficient ways to get the greatest benefit from the time spent with our instruments is a lifelong priority for every player.

One of the most useful tools you can develop is a personal practice book, an individualized collection of technical exercises and musical excerpts that will help you focus your warm-ups and your work, and allow you to learn on several levels at once.

Exercise books for proposed daily practice and warm-up form a special category in the string-players' literature. Different from collections of scales, gatherings of études, or the various "methods" and "schools" that cram the player's library, they are packed full of technical material that is concentrated, focused, and measured out in manageable doses to provide optimum return for the practice time spent.

Before going further, I want to emphasize that the personal practice book is not meant to supplant scales—that "noble, musically basic building material," as Szigeti calls them—nor replace other practicing (études, the literature) so important for all students. But working with examples from actual music is both enjoyable and beneficial, and it keeps significant passages fresh in the mind and hand.

I have been using these books for years with grateful enthusiasm, and I love some of the material I have found in them. The one-string exercises from the Leonard Mogill *Scale Studies for Viola* (G. Schirmer, Inc.), which are based on the J. Hřimaly *Scales for Violin* (Hal Leonard), have been with me for decades. Samuel Lifschey's *Daily Technical Studies for the Violist* (Carl Fischer, out of print) is a treasure chest of original and useful study material. And Leon Pascal's *Technique de l'Alto* (Max Eschig, out of print) contains exercises for independence, crossing, and extensions of the fingers that embody some of the most useful aspects of left-hand control a string player can learn.

But these few examples come from three separate sources—just three out of dozens possible. I don't carry all those books around with me, nor do I work through them all when I practice. I cull material that has a special usefulness, and I try to organize it in a way that will make it even more useful.

Some years ago an excellent violist showed me her own extensive (unpublished) personal book, which she had developed over a period of years. It was divided into the traditional categories of technique, and they were all there: scales, arpeggios, thirds, sixths, octaves, bowing patterns in many rhythms, arpeggiations, bariolage. None of it was excerpts from music. All of it was pure technique.

"The only trouble is that it gets to be addictive," she confided. "There was a period of about three years when I was convinced I couldn't play the viola unless I worked my way through the whole book first, every day. Nowadays I only work through it two or three times a week."

Since playing the whole book took about three hours, it's clear that she had given herself a thorough technical grounding. That kind of persistence can be very beneficial—if you have the time to do it and learn music, too.

I was impressed by her book, and as I thought about it I found that I was being influenced by two other works. In the large bibliography of daily technical studies, these stand out as classics: Carl Flesch's *Urstudien* (Basic Studies), published by Carl Fischer for both violin and viola; and Joseph Szigeti's *A Violinist's Notebook,* published by Gerald Duckworth and Co., Ltd. (out of print). Each approaches the themes of warm-up and efficiency from different points of view.

Flesch's purpose, as he explains in his preface, is to offer a series of maintenance exercises that "comprise the elements upon which the entire general violin technique . . . is built up." He then presents his very useful theoretical analysis, which names and describes the five primary movements of the technique of the left arm, and the six primary movements of the mechanism of the right arm. He follows this discussion with a series of short exercises (none longer than five minutes) that make you use those movements.

These exercises are certainly worth doing, and I think they can be combined beneficially with other approaches. That's where Joseph Szigeti's classic comes in.

A Violinist's Notebook is a beautiful book. Subtitled *200 Music Examples with Notes for Practice and Performance,* it is a distillation of this great violinist and teacher's insight and experience. And what experience he had! The examples come from everywhere in the literature—concertos, orchestra excerpts, second violin parts from quartets; a multiplicity of music, old and new—and all presented with charming scholarship and flair.

"In music," says Szigeti, "there will always remain the element of the unforeseen for which our preparation—however thorough it may have been—will not suffice.

"So why not plunge into some unaccustomed, unexpected challenge at the beginning of each working day, and go on from there, rather than expose your playing organism day by day to the same stimulus (of the same ritualistic warming-up exercises), meeting it, like Pavlov's dog, with the same response?"

The idea of using musical excerpts is not unique to Szigeti, of course. For example, the Edition Peters version of the Hans Sitt *Viola Method* has an appendix of 11 pages of orchestral and chamber-music excerpts. And Harvey Whistler's *Introducing the Positions* series (Rubank Educational Library and Hal Leonard) frequently offers short extracts from the literature to demonstrate newly introduced playing techniques.

But the depth and practicality of Szigeti's comments, combined with his collection of examples, earn his book a special place of honor. Friends of mine who studied with Szigeti say he practiced what he preached; he would even select difficult passages from his musical studies and play them in transposition all over his violin, thus learning both the music and arcane regions of technique simultaneously.

The above examples point toward methods you can use to construct your own personal book. I like to take a mixed approach that combines musical materials for daily study with Flesch's analysis of technical movements—but also covers traditional techniques.

Start by getting organized right from the beginning. Photocopying excerpts and keeping them in a drawer is better than nothing, but usually the drawer gets so crowded you can never find the excerpt you want—I've tried it. Start with a good three-ring binder, one that will lie open on your music stand, with rings large enough to let you turn pages easily. If it's attractive to look at, so much the better. You may be living with this book for a long time, so it's worth doing everything you can to enjoy the association.

Next, label pages for the kind of excerpts you are going to attach to them. I use pieces of paper that I later insert into three-hole plastic sheet covers, but three-hole indexing pages work fine, too. How many will you need? That all depends on how you plan to sort your book. Flesch lists 11 basic technical movements, and I would devote a full page to each one. The customary technical categories of scales, arpeggios, thirds, sixths, and so on can also each get a page; that makes another six or eight. Further subdivision is always possible, but 11 to 20 pages should be a generous start.

And now the lifelong fun begins: filling the book with useful and interesting study material. Look for passages to fill the categories you have defined, photocopy them, and put them in the appropriate place in your book. For example, if you practice the Flesch movements, replace his rather dry gymnastic patterns with musical examples. Instead of doing his exercise IA (Example A), take some chords out of a Bach solo Sonata or Partita, or out of a major concerto (violists will find plenty of examples in Hindemith) and do the movements using that configuration of your hand. In place of abstract patterns for string crossing, use something like the segment from *Aida* (Example B). A longer version of this passage is in my own book. Played on all parts of the bow, at a variety of tempos, it is good for my string crossing and right-wrist flexibility—and when the chance to play *Aida* comes around, I'm ready for it.

Example A

Example B

Musicians taking auditions know that certain excerpts keep showing up over and over again. Why not make the overture to Mozart's *The Marriage of Figaro*, or various sections out of Strauss, part of your daily work? If you wish to fill in the traditional categories of technique, you will have no trouble finding practical musical examples of scales, arpeggios, intervals, and so on. They can even be sorted by key to supplement your scale studies. As your collection grows beyond what is convenient for daily work, the examples can be woven into a larger pattern of scheduling, each being used for perhaps a week at a time and then stored for a future return.

Clearly there is a lot to do, but your efforts will bring you great rewards—and they can also be shared. The whole community of our craft is enriched when individuals are generous with their experience and knowledge. Colleagues can share their collections with each other. Teachers can offer them to their students. Original and interesting anthologies can be published, as Szigeti's was. Building a personal practice book offers benefits that reach out beyond the practice room.

How Fast Is Slow?

8

STRING PLAYING IS COMPOSED of many kinds of learning, each with its own contribution and rate of development. When we practice slowly, these different levels are given time to meet and mingle. Slow practice lets you see the notes coming and also aids in playing them free of uncertainty or tension. As the player, you become aware of what you're doing while you're doing it. You hear sounds clearly, monitor your actions precisely, and give the moving centers in your brain time to sort out complex patterns of posture, balance, and coordination.

Yes, slow practice is good—but it can hold hidden dangers. Sometimes it takes special effort to speed up a passage that has been learned too slowly and heavily. After all, when you practice "The Flight of the Bumblebee" as if it were "The Elephant's Dance," it should come as no surprise if the overweight little creature has trouble taking wing.

Determining the right practice tempo, and working with it effectively, is a valuable practice skill. Every time you pick up an instrument, you face a multitude of choices. The techniques and guidelines that help you find your way through this complexity are precious; they focus your work and give it direction.

And they start before you even pick up your instrument.

Preparation is everything. Before deciding how to practice, first decide what to practice, and why. This triad of choice (what to practice), decision (why that piece or technique), and intention (how to practice it) is the foundation of your work—and it makes your practice conscious.

So the first step in finding the right tempo is to select what you're going to work on and understand why. Formulate your intention. It often helps to say it aloud: "I am practicing this phrase to make it more expressive. . . . I am working on this scale without expression, to make my fingering more fluent. . . . I am taking these eight difficult bars out of context to improve the rapid position shifts."

Unsupervised students often start at the beginning of a piece, play until they make a mistake, and then go back to the beginning. I recommend that you avoid this approach, as it can be counterproductive. To advance your work, identify difficulties and deal with them. Since 80 percent of the technical difficulty in any piece will be concentrated into just 20 percent of the music, find those difficult places, isolate them, and focus on clearing up the problems. This way you'll accelerate your learning of the whole composition.

Let's assume you've selected a passage, you've decided on bowings and fingerings, and you know the objective of your work. Now, decide how to practice it.

You'll need to find the tempo. Through the years, I've found effective guidelines for determining that first slow-practice tempo. These guidelines help establish a middle ground between the extremes of too fast (which scrambles the work) and too slow (which lets it harden into concrete).

First, to pick a speed for practicing a fast passage, find the fastest tempo at which you are certain you can get all the notes, and then slow down to a speed at which you can play without strain. Here's how to find that tempo: Put your instrument in playing position, place your finger on the string on the first note, place your bow on the right string—and don't move. Instead, imagine the passage clearly and accurately. It is your mind that ultimately gives the order to play, so your mind should have a clear idea of what that order means. Imaginatively see, hear, and feel the passage as you mentally place each finger on each note. When you have found the fastest speed at which you can visualize the whole passage without error, you've found a reference tempo. Use a metronome to quantify that tempo and write it down.

The second step is to slow that reference tempo to a speed at which you can play the notes without any tension. This means absolutely no twitching lips, no furrowed forehead, no clenched teeth, no held breath. Play with a stable posture that supports balanced movements, and move efficiently, fluently, and gracefully—without the rigidity of tight muscles. Take conscious charge of these usually unconscious behaviors.

The practice tempo you choose by using this guideline might turn out to be very slow. But because you are gently pressing against your limits, you'll continue to concentrate and feel a sense of forward motion and accomplishment. Again, use a metronome to identify this tension-free tempo, and make a note of it.

The third guideline complements the first and second: No matter how slow the practice tempo, the physical movements used while playing must be quick—quick in the sense of fast, and quick in the sense of alive. Quickness keeps the attention alert and the reflexes crisp. The goal is not to play—or move—as though you were walking under water. Small, precise movements learned with time between them will later join smoothly when the tempo speeds up.

And the tempo will speed up, but not for a while. There are many ways to use a slow tempo for quick practice. Jascha Heifetz used to recommend trilling while playing scales. Trilling in any passage can be a superb way of joining light, deft movements with a slow tempo.

The next consideration is to play with precision. When asked what form of practice he advised for developing evenness in fast running passages, acclaimed violist William Primrose answered, "I advise that such passages be played deliberately unevenly."

The key word here is "deliberately." He advocated changing the rhythms of a passage in an orderly way to "organize . . . confusion in order to gain control over it."

Examples 1 through 11 demonstrate classic practice rhythms that can be used in working on scales or passages.

These orderly combinations (or others of your own invention), chosen deliberately and played with precision, have a beneficial effect on clarity of thought and on control of both hands. In addition to playing them in the usual way, you can also practice these with hands separate (left hand fingering without bow strokes, right hand playing open strings without fingered pitches).

Another effective way to keep both hands lively is to alter the speed of the bow stroke, though the tempo and rhythm do not change, as in Examples 12 through 14. (See the next page.)

Just by scanning this simple sample, you can see that the movements must be ever quicker, even though the beats are at the same pace. (An important consideration here is that the bow strokes should keep the same up-bow and down-bow relationship to string crossings and position changes. For example, if the final version of the piece has one bow stroke per note, then the practice modes should have three strokes—or five, or seven, and so on—because odd-numbered strokes will preserve the pattern of up and down bows.)

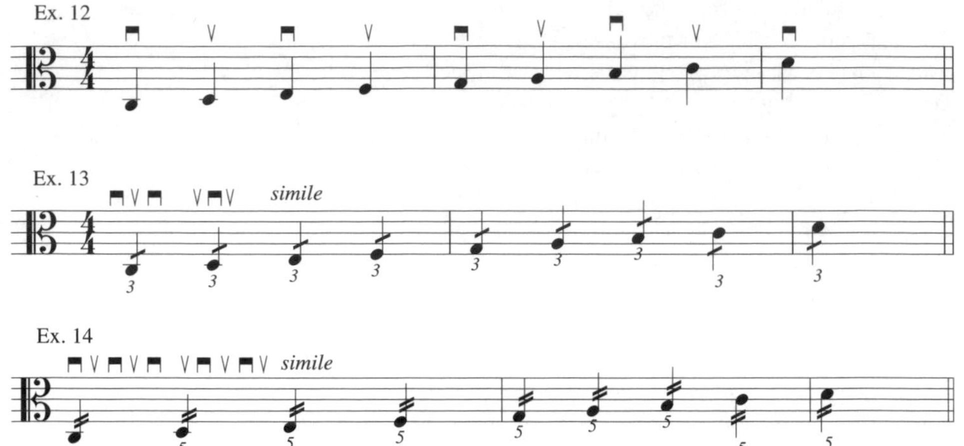

Certainly, there is plenty to do at a slow tempo, and the work is both valuable and fun. It should not be called "grunt work" or treated as if it were the prelude to some distant future gratification. Setting an obtainable goal and then reaching it—even within five minutes—is gratifying. And as we accumulate these small gratifications, we build the knowledge we're seeking.

Picking up the Pace 9

PRACTICE STARTS SLOW; it does not stay slow. Once you've learned a passage or a pattern dependably and comfortably at the starting speed, it's time to bring it up to performance tempo. There are many approaches to this goal. All good approaches will have two traits in common: methodical intention and lively attention.

A metronome or other rhythmic aid can be a helpful companion in this endeavor. Steady of rhythm, patient, noncritical, the metronome is a good partner and a consistent point of reference. I do not believe that practicing with a metronome leads to mechanical playing—at least, not if you don't let it. Inattention and lack of focus can lead to mechanical playing, but not metronome use itself.

A modern electronic rhythm machine provides more options than Maelzel's mechanical invention ever could. It is steady on any surface. It can mark time with clicks, voice, or flashing lights. It can be programmed to play virtually any desired sequence and can be adjusted in very small but clearly quantifiable changes of speed. You can even buy a drum machine and practice with your own virtual big band—it's interesting and less expensive than hiring a pianist to come to your house every day (though that's not bad, either).

Musicians have been working with a variety of timekeepers for ages. Violinist Earl Carlyss once described how the Juilliard String Quartet coped with the rhythmic complexities of a contemporary work: They made four copies of a click track so that each member of the group could work with the same rhythms at home. The click track provided the correct tempos, including accelerandi and ritardandi—in effect, the whole rhythmic shape of the piece. When the ensemble met for rehearsals, each player had a common expectation—in their thoughts and in their practice experience—of how to work together.

One of my own fond memories of working with an electronic practice aid occurred years ago when I was preparing the Dohnányi Serenade for performance. There's plenty to practice in that work, and the third-movement Scherzo is especially challenging. Concert dates were looming, I was feeling pressured and impatient, and I realized that I needed to do something to slow my practice down.

Technology was different then, but it still worked. I transferred an LP recording of the work to a reel-to-reel tape, set the tape machine at half speed, and played along. Because the tape was slow, the recording sounded an octave low in pitch. But I could play along an octave above and my intonation still fit. The clarity and sustained effort of this work were just what I needed, and I learned a lot from my practice partners. Even at half tempo and an octave low, Heifetz, Primrose, and Feuermann played very, very well.

These anecdotes endorse the use of metronomic help in practicing. The most certain way to understand that value is to try it out. There are a few ways to use a metronome for developing velocity in technical practice.

Creeping up: This is the most direct approach to increasing practice speed. Simply increase the metronome setting one, or even a few, clicks at a time, and advance toward the goal in small increments.

Creeping down again: As you gradually speed up a piece or passage, tension can sneak into your playing. If that starts to happen, go back—click by click—to the relatively relaxed earlier practice tempos, then start ascending again. Try to "carry" the relaxed feeling from the slower to the faster pace.

The bounce: In this approach, the tempo goes up and down more rapidly. For example, move the setting up to 12 clicks above your base tempo, then back down to two above, then up to 14 above, then down to four above, and so on. This procedure progresses more quickly than the creeping approach and offers an alternating combination of diagnosis and consolidation.

The influential teacher Demetrius C. Dounis used to advise his pupils to play a work at double tempo and at half tempo. Even if the double tempo is unplayable, it shows exactly where the tangles happen. Even if the half tempo is quite playable, it gives the musician a chance to monitor concentration and control.

Concentration, control, attention, and conscious purpose are the recurrent themes of good practice. These tools of intelligence guide us in our search for efficient and appropriate movement. The great educator Moshé Feldenkrais, who developed the well-known body-movement method, listed four criteria for what he called "coordinated, well-learned action." The first three are absence of effort, absence of inner (muscular) resistance, and uninterrupted breathing.

The fourth criterion, the principle of reversibility, is extremely important and bears some explanation. The ability to stop a movement at any moment and reverse it demonstrates a conscious control over that action, and it shows that you have good postural support for your technique. You should always be moving from one position to another, not falling into it.

We can use this principle as a practice aid at any time. That scale fragment that just went up can also come down. That shift that ascended to a higher position can also descend to a lower one. That passage that you're learning from beginning to end can also be worked on in the other direction.

Most of the techniques we have looked at are what skills-psychologists call the "part-whole" approach, in which small sections are mastered and then joined together. It's a good—even necessary—technique, an antidote to the "play until you mess up" syndrome. When a passage is learned from beginning to end by this method, it is called "chaining."

There's another approach to this process, called "reverse chaining," in which a passage is learned in segments from the end to the beginning. There are beneficial psychological effects from reverse chaining. The practicing musician always knows the next bar better than the one he or she is in. There is a feeling of coming home to what is familiar, rather than a straining toward some distant goal.

All of the practice suggested here has been deliberate, attentive, and methodical. That's the kind of practice that is most productive; it's also the kind that most of us try to run away from as quickly as possible. It's true that the performer must at some time risk a virtuoso bungee leap of faith, a leap that should be made from a platform of solid preparation. Viennese violinist Felix Khuner used to say, "You cannot slowly practice a somersault off the back of a galloping horse." But he would go on to point out that you can practice the separate elements of that move—somersaulting, horseback riding—before you put them all together.

"First you work it over, then you give it the works," said Dylan Thomas about reading poetry in public. The same is true of music. If you work it over well, you will be ready to perform, and the music will rise to meet you.

10 Tools for Better Technique

THE GREAT PIANIST AND COMPOSER Ferruccio Busoni once referred to basic instrumental technique as "a bundle of small picklocks and skeleton keys." The phrase evokes an image of musicians working attentively—with the alert, sensing concentration of focused locksmiths (or quiet safecrackers)—to open the treasures of music, using a bundle of scales, arpeggios, double-stops, and chords. This bundle can be organized into a well-provisioned tool kit through the use of our most powerful practice skill: clear thinking.

No brain, no gain. Clear thinking makes our work more effective. It reduces complex technical challenges to simpler parts: Scale passages are recognized as collections of intervals and position shifts, complex bowings are seen as variations on down bow, up bow, and across-the-strings. The patterns of movement that we spend years learning (technique) are a kind of tool. The principles of how we think about the technique (understanding) become the tool master. And our understanding will lead us to new ways of knowing our instruments and solving musical problems.

Here is a sampling of picklocks and skeleton keys for your own tool kit. They are some of the devices I have found valuable throughout the years. Since I am a violist, these offerings will be most applicable to the "horizontal" instruments, which are held out from the player, parallel to the ground. Players of the "vertical" instruments, such as cellos and basses, will need to adjust some of my descriptions to suit the demands of their instruments.

THE UNFRETTED FINGERBOARD

First, let's take a look at the unfretted fingerboard and learn its landmarks. The unfretted fingerboard is a geography with many latitudes. It stretches from the open fourth string up to the heights of the first string—what Paul Hindemith called "the arctic regions of eternal rosin." To nonplayers, it can look like an expanse without landmarks. But those of us who travel in these regions feel and hear the markers that guide the way.

We can *think* the landmarks, too. By imagining a fictitious pattern of 24 semitone frets across the open strings, we delineate 100 tempered pitches that compose our path. It's certainly true that there are more notes in the roadway—untempered notes, bent notes, slides, and so on—and we have to know them as well. But with modest effort, it is possible to make organized contact with each one of these 100 basic tones. Here is a streamlined approach:

There is just one chromatic scale comprising all 12 semitones. Play a two-octave chromatic scale on each string, starting on an open string, and you will have touched every tempered note on the instrument.

There are just two whole-tone scales. They are positioned a semitone apart and never meet—like bishops on opposite color squares in chess. Play two two-octave whole-tone scales on each string and you will touch every tempered note on the fingerboard. (Since all diatonic scales contain a whole-tone sequence, this practice transfers widely to many other applications.)

The three diminished-seventh chords travel by express around the circle of fifths and often figure prominently in modulations. Play three two-octave diminished-seventh chords on each string and you will have played every tempered note on the fingerboard. We're usually asked to go that high only on the I and II strings. It is a big reach to ascend that far on the III and IV strings, but when we do take this path, we will have played every note on the fingerboard.

In the search for graceful and efficient fingerings, it's always useful to think in terms of hand groupings. Thinking of groups, rather than individual notes, makes it easier to find patterns. The hand groupings and quick position changes in Example 1 work to minimize awkward string crossing and help maintain the very quick tempo.

Example 1

One of my favorite examples of a hidden pattern is a short scale from the viola part of John Adams' opera *The Death of Klinghoffer*. It's just 16 notes long, ten of them with accidentals. The first time I saw it, someone had cluttered it with unnecessary markings:

Example 2

After I looked at it for awhile, the regular tetrachord pattern emerged:

Example 3

Even theoretically correct fingerings have to be practiced, but this discovery saved some work. Several of my colleagues thanked me for finding this particular fingering. But Natasha Vershilova, my stand partner during this opera, looked at the way the hand goes backward while the scale ascends, wriggled her fingers in my face, and said with a smile, "This fingering is like a bad dream."

HAND GROUPINGS

I came by my fondness for hand groupings while studying in Paris with Leon Pascal. He had developed a technical practice based on broken chords, which he assigned to all of his students. It emphasized arpeggiations, with the hand keeping the framework of an octave.

Example 4

Pascal's inspiration came from the now-rare Edward Nadaud scale system. In his 1928 book *Gammes Practiques pour Violon* (Editions Costallat), the broken chords were one among a variety of virtuoso practices. Pascal expanded the arpeggios into a system and added variations and practice approaches for both hands. In my personal practice book, I find 97 variations that he assigned. They are similar to the multiple variations to be found in Ševčík or other works of that type, but they are applied to arpeggios.

TO SHIFT OR NOT TO SHIFT

Technically efficient shifting usually occurs on one or more of the following occasions: a change of rhythm, a change of bow, a change of string, on an open string, or on the smallest available interval. Watching for these five instances can help you find some unexpected ways of slithering around the fingerboard, as in this minimalist, three-octave, almost no-shift scale. (See Example 5.) This example is an extreme case of the fifth principle. It can be quite handy, although it is more useful in expressive passages than fast ones.

Example 5

GAINED AND LOST BOW

An understanding of gained and lost bow is important to stringed-instrument musicians. Most players experience the effect for years without consciously identifying it. But consciously understanding the phenomenon can help alleviate the feeling of your bow "going against gravity."

When a continuous bow stroke is drawn across all four strings following the curve of the bridge (down bow from player's left to right, up bow from right to left), the bow feels longer because a small part of the bow is used again with each individual string crossing. This is referred to as gained bow. By contrast, when a continuous bow stroke is drawn counter to the curve of the bridge (up bow from left to right, down bow from right to left), the bow feels shorter, because parts of the bow are not used at all. This is called lost bow.

It is not always possible to conform bowing to all the principles of ease; we have to practice everything. But by staying aware of the concept of gained and lost bow, we find that it applies to much more than arpeggios and slurred scales. The phenomenon influences all string changes to some degree. For example, it is well known that string crossings with separate bows are more comfortable played down bow on the left-hand string and up bow on the right-hand string. This too is a gained-bow effect.

Keeping this in mind, one can make the following viola solo from Milhaud's *Christophe Colomb* slightly less awkward by slurring the first two notes to get to the more efficient pattern, and then slurring the last two notes to get back again. (See Example 6, next page.)

Example 6

Rossini always asks us to do the difficult things. There is a page of triplets from the viola part of *An Italian Girl in Algiers* that can be very difficult if approached note by note. Organized thinking makes a big difference. It is possible to group the fingers in a way that maintains a consistent framework of the hand, equalizes gained and lost bow every six notes, and keeps the bowing pattern consistent on two strings.

A few recommended publications bolster the concepts discussed here. Percival Hodgson's *Motion Study and Violin Bowing* (American String Teacher's Association) contains a discussion of gained and lost bow, complete with complex diagrams. I recommend that you read it. But I recommend even more strongly that you experiment with the bow and identify its characteristics.

Many wonderful discussions of bowing can be found in our music-teaching literature, including Carl Flesch's *The Art of Violin Playing*, Book I (Carl Fischer); Ivan Galamian's *The Principles of Violin Playing* (Shar Products Co); and Samuel Applebaum's *The Way They Play* (Paganiniana Publications), especially in the Preface to Volume IV.

Any musician wishing to pursue the concept of hand groupings should consult Primrose's scale book, *Technique Is Memory* (Oxford University Press), which applies the technique of hand groupings to scales, as well as Robert Gerle's *The Art of Practising the Violin* (Stainer and Bell), which contains a systematic table of finger patterns.

These are just a few of the guidelines and principles that can help us organize our technical tool kit. The mind directs the hands, and the hands inform the mind. When practice is viewed as an experimental approach to understanding, it is more satisfying, more effective, and more fun.

Pizzicato: The Other Way to Play

11

HARPISTS AND GUITARISTS SPEND almost all their working time playing pizzicato. They make their music—and their careers—by plucking strings. Those of us who activate our strings with horsehair and wood tend to give less attention to this special skill. Our practice time is already quite committed. Our bows keep us busy.

Unfortunately, this lack of attention to pizzicato can often be heard. All but the greatest orchestras have offered unison pizzicatos that sounded more like a string of firecrackers than a resonant strum. Gentle, lutelike accompaniments to romantic arias are frequently shattered by an inadvertent "Bartók snap." And the plucked chords of Brahms' G Major Violin Sonata can sound as if the soloist were trying to tear the strings off the instrument. The "Rain" Sonata suddenly becomes a hailstorm.

When a composer asks for the distinctive sound of pizzicato, it is up to the performer to fulfill that request with as much imagination and skill as is given to any other aspect of our craft. Most pizzicato effects are not athletically demanding, but all music is musically demanding. Just a few minutes a day spent practicing some of the special effects of plucking strings on violin, viola, cello, or bass can give a remarkable variety of results and can provide a repertoire of skills on ready reserve for the future. (In fairness, it should be mentioned that many bass players often learn this when they are young. Their frequent crossover into jazz—where the bow is less commonly used than the plucking fingers—gives them practical experience with this kind of technique.)

There is a lot to think about and experiment with in pizzicato; it has as many dimensions as bowing. Where the string is plucked will affect tone, though the traditional area near the end of the fingerboard and over the ebony—away from rosin—has the practical advantage of keeping the plucking finger from getting sticky and the bowed part of the string from getting oily.

Which part of the finger does the plucking is also important. For example, a fleshy contact of the finger creates a much warmer, less metallic sound than does the fingernail. Some years ago, Maestro Josef

Krips tried to make this point during a rehearsal of the San Francisco Symphony, when he shouted at the orchestra, "Play with the flesh from your finger, not with the horn! You are scratching like chickens in a chicken stable!" (By "horn" Krips meant fingernail.) Language barrier or no, Krips made his point and the pizzicatos became warmer. He also inadvertently released tension during a difficult rehearsal with the expression "chicken stable," which brought forth a great burst of laughter from the orchestra—even Krips saw the humor, when it was explained to him.

In contemporary music, composers often ask for a variety of special pizzicato effects: the flick of fingernails against the strings, for example, or the famous above-mentioned "Bartók snap," in which the string is plucked extra hard—actually it is pinched upward and released downward—so it will slap against the fingerboard. It is always right to do what a composer asks, as long as the request does not injure player or instrument. Imaginative and proactive preparation of special effects can lead to musical benefits in all kinds of music. Each finger can be explored for its own particular capabilities.

Take the thumb, for example. It is the thickest, fleshiest, most powerful finger. Harpists and guitarists depend on it. But most violinists and violists do not use it for pizzicato, and I think the same is true for cellists.

My own experiments have made me quite fond of my thumb. With the viola held in normal playing position and the thumb pointed toward the scroll, the fleshiest part of the thumb comes in easy contact with the string and the stroke can follow the arc of the bridge. It is possible to release a string so that it vibrates in a sideways direction, parallel with, rather than perpendicular to, the fingerboard. This can produce a ringing and resonant sound with less possibility of extraneous buzzing or an unwanted snap. And the thumb is clearly the digit of choice when the instrument is held *a la guitarra*.

Most violinists and violists first learn to use the index finger for pizzicato, though cellists and bassists are usually taught to use the middle finger first. I remember that at my first violin lesson, decades ago, I was taught—along with other useful things, such as never to rest my violin case upside down—to brace my right thumb against the corner of the fingerboard near the E string and to pluck each of the open strings and call them by name. I now think that was a good idea, though at the time I was disappointed: I had wanted to use my bow. Still, to have a physical sense of where the strings are and how they can be sounded is a nice way to start violin lessons.

And the technique continues to be useful. Bracing the thumb against the fingerboard can give extra stability to the right hand. I know of one concertmaster of a major orchestra who used to ask that all string sections play that way. He thought the stability increased rhythmic control.

Personally, I think that once the location of the strings has been learned, a greater flair and freedom can be attained by reaching for them with a motion through the air. And that motion can come from the finger joints, from the wrist, or even like a peck from the elbow. (I've seen this last technique done in a very rapid passage, and I've heard it strongly advocated, though I find it uncomfortable whenever I try it.)

The index and middle fingers can work together, too. Powerful pizzicato tones can be produced by plucking single notes with both fingers side by side. And the fingers can also work in sequence; in rapid passages, index and middle finger can pluck alternately, like a little man running across the strings. But this last technique needs extra practice. It requires great attention to the evenness of the stroke, the balance of the tone production, and the maintenance of steady tempo.

While we are working with more than one finger at a time, we can continue to add fingers. There are passages in some of Richard Strauss' music (in *Elektra*, for example) where he asks that each note of a series of quickly repeated triplets be played with a different finger: 1-2-3, 1-2-3, 1-2-3. In more than two decades of performing this opera, I have never yet heard the triplets sound even—but perhaps that's what the composer intended.

The recognition that chords do not always have to be strummed or arpeggiated is important and useful. They can be plucked with each string getting a finger of its own. In fact, that's my preferred solution to the problem of the pizzicato chords in the Brahms sonata mentioned earlier. With one plucking finger on each string played, the whole chord can be released at once. Either a lift of the hand or a rolling away of the wrist will produce a full, simultaneous ringing of the strings.

The effectiveness of several of the preceding techniques is influenced by whether or not the bow is being held in the right hand at the same time. In actual performance, there is not always enough time to put the bow down and pick it up again between plucked note and stroked note. Adjustments have to be made for the change of balance in the hand and the oscillations that are sometimes set up when the bow is held loosely. In extended orchestral pizzicato passages, playing with the bow down is often requested by the conductor or the section leader, because it gives the right hand more freedom. And it can be especially important to play extended passages with the bow down when the orchestra is in the pit. Pity the poor singer on stage who tries to single out the conductor's baton from the middle of a mob of violin and viola bows wagging like threatening sticks.

The left hand is also important in pizzicato. Firm stopping of the string and a healthy vibrato can strengthen the tone of plucked notes. A device frequently used by guitarists and harpists carries over to the violin family: Harmonics will ring like open strings if the stopping finger is lifted just after the string is plucked.

And the left hand can do its own pizzicato as well. Ensemble players know that using the left hand to pluck a note or two just before a quick entrance with the bow can often save effort and help accuracy. This device can be taken much further, all the way to the virtuoso trick of doing whole passages of left-hand pizzicato. The technique can be done in two ways. The more common way is by preplacing the fingers on the string and then plucking it as the fingers are pulled off to the side. Descending scales are done this way, with the fingers snapped off in sequence and an occasional individual bowed note or right-hand pizzicato thrown in to keep the scale alive. The other way—which can only be heard when the audience is extremely quiet and attentive—is simply to thump fingers down on their notes. This technique, which is called "hammering on" by guitarists, makes short ascending scales possible.

Virtuosos have a big stake in making sure that their audiences recognize their virtuosity. Everyone I've ever seen play these effects makes a point of holding the bow far away from the instrument—high, high in the air—to get the point across. But who can blame them? Getting the point across is one of the responsibilities of any performer. And composers don't always make that easy to do.

For example, some music asks for a rhythmic/durational difference between sixteenth-, eighth-, and quarter-note pizzicatos. The task is tricky; all plucked notes tend to fade quickly, and the higher the pitch of the note, the shorter its life expectancy. But it is possible to use vibrato to add to the ring and duration of a pizzicato note. And the movement of the right hand can also help a note seem longer or shorter. By lengthening or shortening the follow-through of the right hand, one can suggest to the audience how long a note is supposed to sound, and they will hear it that way. We perform for the eyes as well as the ears, and we should do everything we can to help an audience hear a piece the way we want them to.

There are still more ways that the two hands can work together. At one spot in *Petroushka,* the viola section is asked to play a series of repeated D's above middle C very rapidly. I've heard this played quite convincingly on the open D string, by alternating pizzicato between the index or third finger of the right hand and the third finger of the left hand. I play this passage by stopping a unison D on the G string below open D and an octave D on the A string above, aiming my index finger toward the scroll with my right hand upside down over the fingerboard (an inversion of the classic pointing finger), and then whipping my finger back and forth across the D string, hitting it with each sideways stroke. This works well, and the stopped strings on either side ensure that any accidents or slightly missed strokes will still sound at the right pitch.

Perhaps the most fanciful solution to this particular technical problem that I have ever seen was in the early days of my career, when I was in the Oakland Symphony. Our principal violist was Germain Prevost, who for many years was the violist of the Pro Arte String Quartet. Prevost was very conscientious, and he pondered this passage from *Petroushka* seriously, even though it was not very exposed. (All the violas are playing, and the cellos have their own pizzicato low B and D at the same time.) Still, Prevost wanted to do it right. After several days of thought, he arrived at the following approach: He tuned his G string up to D, held the instrument like a cello, braced his right thumb against one side of the fingerboard and his left thumb against the other, and plucked the two separate strings, alternating right and left hands. The repeated D's came out loud and clear when he demonstrated them to us backstage. And the whole procedure may have added to the visual interest of our performances. But it did seem as if he spent half the piece tuning the G string up and then another third of the piece tuning it back down to G. Having a second viola available might have been more practical, but his way was certainly lively to watch.

All kinds of results are possible with personal experimentation. It's fun, and it's worth the effort. When a student gets so carried away that he or she begins to develop calluses on the pizzing fingers, all a teacher has to do is drop a reminder that interesting effects are possible with the bow, too.

And those also have to be practiced.

12 Bow Explorations

THE BOW LOOKS SIMPLE TO THE EYE, but to the hand it is a rich territory filled with many textures, directions, and responses. By entering this landscape in a spirit of playful adventure, you can launch journeys of exploration and discovery that will deepen your knowledge and improve your skills.

Through the years I have gathered practice devices that help this exploration. These practices allow us to observe and feel the bow work we are focused on. They can be adapted to any level of player—from early student to professional—with good results.

The first is tapping. To appreciate the range of balance and bounce along the full length of the bow, start by tapping the bowhair on a string. Place the tip of your bow on the lowest-pitched string of your instrument, then lift the bow a little bit above the string and start tapping. Notice how much spring you feel as the bow "wants" to rebound.

Continue tapping as you slowly move the contact point on the bow toward the frog. Note the change in the bounce, and your need for increasingly more right-hand help as you go up bow toward the heavier end of the stick. Try for as much control as possible as you maintain an even, regular tapping. Keep the right hand free of unnecessary tension, and keep the bow close to the string.

The late Charles Siani—principal bass of the San Francisco Opera orchestra for many years, and a very effective teacher—used to tell his students that once they had tapped in this way, they would know everything they needed to know about the bow. It was an exaggeration, but it got them thinking.

Another exploration that uses the spring of the upper half of the bow is what I call the "tremble." Instead of tapping, drop the bow onto the string from a height of two to four inches, creating a ricochet bounce. It may take a few tries to find the right height and the right location on the bow. Once you do, start a very slow down bow that encourages a small ricochet to continue. The right hand must hold the bow delicately, and the arm must move slowly so that traction between string and bow causes the bounce to continue.

This is great practice for developing a light bow hold and a steady arm—and it helps you learn control of an effect that nerves might cause when you don't want it.

The next tip focuses on the expression *son filé*, French for "spun-out sound." Originally borrowed from vocal technique, the expression means a sustained, singing sound—the heart of expressive string playing. "Everyone worries about spiccato," violinist Felix Khuner once said, "but the sustained legato tone is what's important. That's where the money's at! Once you have it, you can cut it as short or as long as you want."

To approach son filé, I teach a practice that I call the "Bow Stretcher." It doesn't really stretch the bow, or deform it in any way, but it does stretch the thinking of the player. It teaches a precise mental skill for monitoring and controlling a bow stroke as it is happening.

Play a series of even, paired strokes, making each successive down/up pair a little bit longer in time—and slower in motion—than the preceding one. To do this, set a metronome at 60 (one second per click is a good beginning setting) and place the bow at its midpoint on the lowest open string of your instrument. Play several pairs of down/up bow strokes at the rate of one click per stroke. At the start, use only as much bow length as you feel you need; you'll be using the entire length soon enough.

Begin adding clicks, one click at a time. Use the same length of bow for each down/up pair, but make each pair one click longer than the preceding one. Example 1 shows the first eight pairs in musical notation.

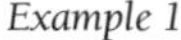

Example 1

In order to keep the bow moving steadily and evenly, you need to think ahead by counting clicks and mentally distributing them along the bow length. For example, think: "At eight clicks per stroke, I'll have four in the lower half and four in the upper half. At nine, four in each half, with number five right at the midpoint. Ten will be five upper half plus five lower half . . ." and so on.

The Bow Stretcher is versatile: You can practice it as a sustained scratch (good for control, hard on the ears). You can play it on each of the four open strings, on the three double-string combinations, and in wave patterns across two or more strings (a living lesson in gained and lost bow).

Also, the concept can be reversed to facilitate faster bow strokes: Start with the eight-click pairs and then deduct one click at a time while continuing to use the full length of the bow.

The Bow Stretcher can be tiring, so use it sparingly—two or three times a week, with a gradual building to the longest strokes, is a good start. Even with a modest beginning, the return to more "normal" bow speeds can immediately feel and sound freer.

Next come the techniques of drifting and rolling. The point of contact between the bow and the string has a strong effect on tone production. So does the tilt of the bow and the spread of the hairs. Is the bow near the bridge, over the fingerboard, or somewhere in between? Does the tilt of the bow hold the hairs in full, flat contact with the string, or is it angled steeply so that one side of the hairs makes more contact than the other? These questions can be answered and experienced by the practices I call "Intentional Drifting" and "Rolling the Bow."

Intentional Drifting: The distance from the bridge to the fingerboard can be measured in widths of bow hair; there are five or six widths on the violin and viola, more on the lower instruments. Teacher and writer Samuel Applebaum called these divisions "lanes." Like good freeway drivers, players need to learn to make smooth lane changes. Smoothly change lanes from sul ponticello to sul tasto as you draw long bows. We can also jump lanes (which freeway drivers should not try), so practice quick, distant changes as well, moving from the hoarse sounds near the bridge to the transparency near the fingerboard, and back again.

Rolling the Bow: Hear and feel the tonal effects of the angle of the bow hairs on the string by rolling the bow during long strokes—tilt the stick toward your nose, then away, then back again (see Example 2). Do this repeatedly, noting the changes of sensation in your right hand, and the changes of sound from your instrument.

Example 2

Now let's discuss "the Bite." The instant at which tone begins on any stringed instrument is an important and delicate moment. But the instant just before that moment is even more important. During the instant just before playing, the player needs to imagine what the tone sounds like—and what it must feel like.

Through years of practice and experience, you develop a repertoire of movements that are predictive of the sounds they produce. Eventually, you will learn to feel the difference—ahead of time—between slither and scratch (and everything in between).

The Bite helps make this clear. To start the Bite, stop all the strings by placing one left-hand finger on each one. This should not be a strenuous positioning; a simple stack of minor sixths will do—fingers 1-2-3-4 on strings IV-III-II-I on violin and viola.

This dampens the natural ringing of the open strings so we can hear more clearly. With your strings dampened, place the midpoint of the bow on one of the lower-pitched strings. Use the arm position that Ivan Galamian called the "natural square," with right angles at the elbow, between the bow and the forearm, and where the bow crosses the strings. Later, you'll try the Bite using all parts of the bow between the point and the frog, but when starting out you should concentrate your efforts on the middle of the bow.

Next, without making a sound, feel the contact between the bow and the strings. Feel the elasticity of the hairs when you press the wood down and then release it, feel the traction grip of the hairs on the string when you apply the bow firmly, feel how it is possible to move the string without releasing it.

Once you feel this traction, important learning occurs: When the bow is firmly on the string, you can move it with a small, quick motion of the fingers, down bow or up bow. The goal is to release the string with a small pop of sound—as if the bow is plucking the string.

There are ways to fake this sound, but not the movement. For this exercise, the small, quick release should not come from the arm (the elbow) or the hand (the wrist). It should come from a quick, small movement of the fingers. "It's like scratching a little itch," one of my students once said. Sometimes the bow will skid, sometimes it will scratch. Immediate success is not the goal; you are exploring possibilities. The broader your repertoire of experience, the better you will predict a sound before you make it.

Practice the Bite just a few minutes a day, every day. When it feels under control, you can use it to practice scales, passages of separate notes, as spiccato preparation, and for staccato. The sensitivities you learn from this practice will enable you to start a full tone as soon as the bow moves. This skill is important to many kinds of strokes. Martelé, collé, spiccato, and legato all benefit from it.

The examples I have suggested are part of a lifetime program of explorations—in music study, instrument study, and body awareness. The full spectrum of string sound, from flautando to pesante, lives somewhere between whoosh and crunch. Doing these practices—sometimes closer to whoosh, sometimes closer to crunch—will help you discover the regions of tone available through your bow.

13 Vibrato

STUDENTS SOMETIMES ASK how to start vibrato—that is, should one start on pitch and then move lower first, or move upward? The simplest answer is that the vibrato should be downward from the intended musical pitch. The reason is that the highest tone draws the most attention to itself. Vibrate above the note, and you will sound sharp. Vibrate up to that note, and you will sound expressive.

That's the simple answer. It is in keeping with the general taste and practice of our times, and it is true enough to take you a long way. But vibrato is not simple. It is a very personal mode of musical expression, nuance, and inflection. If you watch artists on videotape, you will see that they all vibrate below the pitch—but what a variety of expression they have! What you do (and, by extension, how you do it) depends on the particular music you are playing, and on your relation to that music.

For instance, though we all love the singing quality of a sustained, note-to-note vibrato, some musical sections are expressed best with no vibrato at all (the so-called "white tone"). In others, you can achieve emphasis by starting without vibrato and then bringing it in for part of the line. There is an effect that I call "wild vibrato"—often heard in the work of jazz singers—in which a note is started dead, with vibrato gradually added until it oscillates around the original pitch. You wouldn't use this device in Mozart or Beethoven, but in 20th-century music there are places where it can be just the thing.

Vibrato comes in many combinations of speed and amplitude, so there are many ways to play it. All of these ways are discovered through personal experimentation. The exercises recommended in books and methods are helpful guides to that experimentation; they are not guaranteed "how-to" prescriptions.

Though there is no single correct kind of vibrato, some kinds are certainly used more often than others. I advise my students to stick with the idea of moving lower than the pitch while continuing to experiment with the various components of their own vibrato motion. This ultimately adds more colors to their palette of sounds and enlarges their music making.

Tremolo 14

TREMOLO IS AN IMPORTANT AND DIFFICULT stroke, but most of us don't think about it until we have to play it. Although it seldom occurs in the solo or chamber-music repertoire, pages of tremolo can crop up in major symphonic works of the 19th and early 20th centuries. I have seen highly developed players, smooth and well-practiced in most of their skills, trying to tremolo from the shoulder, stiffening the entire arm. And later they say, "I've never had to play tremolo for half an hour before. Nobody ever taught me how to do it."

Tremolo has to be learned, like every other bow stroke. There are efficient ways that need to be recognized and practiced. There are inefficient ways that need to be recognized and avoided. It is an advanced technique that builds on other developed skills.

One reference work that does mention tremolo is *The Violin Guide,* by Stefan Krayk (American String Teachers Association). Krayk offers this helpful description: "Very fast, short detaché strokes at the point of the bow. The arm must not tighten. Because of the speed of this stroke, the movements are small and are done almost entirely by the fingers and hand from the wrist."

Krayk's definition and advice are accurate and helpful, and I would like to expand on them. The following pedagogical and practice devices, which help focus attention on the right blend of movements, have been very useful in my own practice and in my work with students.

Rest the right forearm on a table or other flat surface, with the arm touching the surface from elbow to wrist. Tap the fingertips against the surface as if they were all striking the space bar of a computer keyboard (or an old-fashioned typewriter). Now do a similar movement, but think of the knuckles as tapping a surface above the hand, as if the imaginary space bar were in the air over the table (I'll call this Movement 1).

When this has been experimented with for awhile, it will be time to go to the air. Hold the right wrist with the left hand, pronate the right hand as if it were holding a bow on one middle string (of whatever kind of bowed instrument you play), and do Movement 1.

In Movement 2, the hand moves upward from the wrist and the thumb and middle finger make a loose circle, as if they were holding and ringing a small dinner bell. When the motion feels familiar and relaxed, the left hand can gradually release its grip until the right wrist is fully free.

These small motions of the wrist and fingers can now be tried holding the bow. The least fatiguing tremolo allows great freedom to the third and fourth fingers of the right hand. I recommend that they come off the stick as the hand pronates. Let the first two fingers do the work.

In all bowing, the relationship between the thumb and the fingers holding the bow is crucial. There must be enough firmness to hold the bow securely, but not so much that the wrist stiffens and cannot move flexibly. Exploring the various possibilities of security with absence of unnecessary tension is one of the major goals of all bowing practice.

Here is another device, straight from the professional front lines: You can make sure that the movements are coming from your wrist by resting your right forearm on your knee—when you can do so and still reach the string you're playing on. Even in performance, this can be a useful way to rest the arm while still playing. (In fact—don't tell anyone!—you can sometimes help the tremolo by shaking your leg. This is fun to try at home, and it can be useful in the pit orchestra. But I don't recommend it for the stage. It looks funny.)

These suggestions are much easier to demonstrate than to describe, but they will, I hope, prove helpful. Whatever devices we use, we always need to remember the importance of tone. Even in tremolo we try for tone, especially since it can be very difficult for us to hear ourselves in orchestra playing. When we have practiced well, we know we are making a good contribution.

PART TWO

COUNSEL & GUIDANCE

Becoming a professional musician means being dependable and being prepared. Orchestral musicians are expected to show up on the right day, at the right time, at the right building, wearing the right clothes, ready to sit down and play exactly the right notes at exactly the right moment, day after day. That requires a high degree of dependability. In this section, you'll find guidelines for professional and nonprofessional alike, including these all-important points: Allow extra time for traffic. Have spares of the tools that you need for your instrument. Bring along snacks and anything special that you need to take care of yourself.

Last but not least, find a place where you can sleep in between performances. During one particularly heavy opera season, when we were performing Wagner's Ring Cycle, *I was walking through the Opera House between services and went backstage to talk to one of the stagehands. And there, lying on the sloping rake of the darkened stage, I found all 18 stagehands, taking a nap.*

Be Prepared 15

THE CHRISTMAS, CHANUKAH, AND NEW YEAR holiday seasons can be the busiest times of the year for working musicians. In addition to the joys and efforts of shopping, gift giving, and celebrating, an active string player might also fill the days—and nights—with the *Messiah*, the *Nutcracker*, and a New Year's *Night in Old Vienna*.

Along with this harvest of work and income can go hours and hours of driving, short nights of sleep, and meals eaten in a rush. In one familiar word: stress. Heavy scheduling intensifies the demands that professional musicians always face, demands that go beyond good musicianship. Playing well is just the beginning; to be successful, a musician has to be dependable. That means being organized and self-directed enough to meet all requirements while staying rested, healthy, and positive.

These are high standards, but they can be met with the help of forethought and preparation, which smooth the way toward periods of intense work.

Through the years, my colleagues and I have found many useful devices for managing our busy musical lives. They all derive from this important theme: When you plan ahead, you make things easier for yourself later.

BE HEALTHY AND RESTED

Taking good care of yourself always comes first. Being in good health and good shape—in your body and on your instrument—forms the foundation for musical success. This is especially true when the workload is heavy. If you try to dive into a busy schedule after a break (a vacation, an illness, a life emergency), you risk soreness and injury.

You lessen that risk by coming to work with toned and practiced muscles. You further lessen it by warming up and cooling down effectively. Follow the principle "heat before playing, ice after playing." You can do this while you commute—a real time-saver. Even in temperate weather, consider wearing gloves while you drive. You can wear heat wraps on the way to the gig and cold packs on the way home.

All our lives we hear these bits of good advice: Practice, eat well, exercise, get enough sleep. Fine counsel, all of it. If you follow the advice conscientiously, you will find that each of these endeavors is a study in itself. I recommend the study, though I also recognize that this is not the place to prescribe a diet or plan an exercise program. You will find your own. But there is one line of learning that deserves special mention: conscious relaxation, the intentional recognition and release of unnecessary tension in your body. Having an alert, calm mind in a healthy, relaxed body is a state of being. Entering this state sometimes requires special skill.

RELAX

Good instrumental instruction should include training in techniques of self-scanning and tension release. The practice of these techniques should be part of daily life—relaxation and stress-reduction skills offer ever-increasing benefits when they are used through the years. Eliciting the relaxation response, using progressive relaxation or autogenic training, or experimenting with other exercises in the mind-body relationship that often get lumped together under the word *meditation*—all of these have a place in life and in music.

If you need a quick stress reliever, here's a simple one. I call it "the secret smile and the whispered *ahh*." First, sense the corners of your mouth and eyes. Then let go of any tension that you find there. Feel that you are smiling a secret smile. While you imagine this secret smile, whisper—or quietly sigh—"ahhh," as if you were trying to fog up a mirror.

That's all there is to it. With these simple actions you have relaxed the two most immediate body responses to stress: a tensed face and tightened breathing. The subtle physical sensations are easeful and positive. Most people feel beneficial effects the first time they try this.

CARE FOR YOUR TOOLS

Active players know the importance of a bow that still pulls sound, strings that hold their pitch, and an instrument that is free of mysterious buzzes. Take proper care of your instrument, and it will take care of you. Is your instrument free of wolf tones and rattles? Are your strings fresh, and do you have a spare set in the case? Has your bow been rehaired recently? You can save yourself future worries by having your instrument adjusted well ahead of any period of intense work.

The same holds true for your car: A dependable set of wheels is extremely important for musicians on the move. Anyone who's going to do a lot of driving in December should have the car safety checked in November. Good brakes, good tires, and a reliable battery and starter will eliminate many automotive worries and emergencies.

PLAN AHEAD

Once your car has been made safe, it can be outfitted to serve as your base station during the coming weeks. Spare yourself those rushed last-minute searches. Plan ahead, make a list of what you'll need, and provide it in advance.

Do you wear glasses? Keep an extra pair in the car. Do you take medicines? Keep a spare supply there, too.

Have you been asked to bring your own stand to a job? Put two in the car trunk ahead of time—one for you and one for the colleague who forgot. Include stand lights and power cables, too, if you have them. I have not yet found battery-operated stand lights that are bright enough for me, but if they work for you, use them—and pack some backup batteries as well.

You know you're going to be asked to complete W-4, W-9, and I-9 forms; fill them out ahead of time and keep them in your car, or in your case.

You also know that you'll have to sit on often uncomfortable folding chairs, so keep a seat cushion and a back support in your car. They'll help make those long seated hours more livable. If it's not too much hassle for you to bring your own chair, do so.

Advance preparation can also extend to your cooking. If you prepare double meals now and freeze half for later, you'll thank yourself in the future. You also may want to outfit your car with a cooler, or even a small refrigerator that plugs into the cigarette lighter. You deserve a leisurely meal between services, but that's not always possible. And you might not want to depend on fast food. Sometime when you're trapped in traffic (it happens!) a handy, thoughtfully prepared snack or sandwich can make all the difference.

KEEP AN EYE ON TIME

Another valuable tool is a good alarm clock. It can protect you from oversleeping and help you take short naps on busy days. Use a clock that can be set precisely and that won't stop ringing until you turn it off. And if you've promised to do something at a specific time, write the promise on a Post-it note, stick it on the clock, and set the alarm.

DRESS FOR SUCCESS

Think ahead about your clothing. Adjust your performance dress for comfort and ease of playing. In our society, women in the music world seem to have more leeway than men about the details of how they dress; they can find ways to be comfortable. Men have to finagle more, but there are things you can do. I wear lightweight, slightly oversized performance clothing, and I have had a pleat put in the back center seam of my jackets. Now there is no fabric tug when I raise my arms to play the viola. Gussets under the arms can also have this effect.

Once your clothes are comfortable, they should also be clean and neat. We are hired to play well and to look good. Well-dressed, well-groomed musicians add to the festivity of the occasion. Leave the grunge to the rockers—unless it's specifically requested.

Practice thinking ahead and you'll find that early preparation always eases later stress. Anything helpful that you do ahead of time is a gift that you make to your future self. The gift will be appreciated, so be generous. It's in the holiday spirit.

Contract Tips for the Gigging Player

16

Dear Mr. Heifetz,
Please come to my birthday party.
(P.S. Please don't forget to bring your violin.)

THERE IS MUSIC FOR ALMOST EVERY KIND of human gathering, and musicians are often asked to play it—for free. Through the learning years, as a player's skill grows, the number of requests to play at special events grows, too. Students are asked to play in school and in church; schoolmates are asked to play at dances; friends are asked to play at weddings.

It is natural and healthy for musicians to spread goodwill while gaining experience and reputation. But there comes a moment (different for everyone) when the process turns professional. Money is offered—or asked for—and then new dimensions of mutual obligation are established between musicians and their listeners.

When that starts to happen, both sides are best served by making clear agreements about the forthcoming exchange. How much music is expected? How much money will be paid? What else do both parties need to know? When musicians agree to come out of their practice rooms and play for pay in front of others, the arrangements and expectations need to be precise. And they need to be written down. That way there is less chance of anyone being disappointed.

Making agreements—and sticking to them—is one of the most important human activities. I have heard many people express annoyance and impatience with written agreements: "Why be so formal?" "Can't people trust one another?" "Can't business be done honorably with a simple handshake?" Anyone who can shake hands with honor can sign with honor. Agreements should be written because the human mind is complex and human memory is fallible. (Have you ever misplaced your keys? Mixed up appointments you hadn't written down?)

The other reason to commit the agreement to writing is that the different parties involved can come to different conclusions at the end of a conversation, without even realizing it. I was once present at the end of a business discussion between a friend and his mother. It went like this: "Well, that sounds pretty good, Mom. Let's write it up." "Oh no, dear. We don't have to write anything. I'm your mother; I trust you." "Mom, don't trust me! We've been talking for an hour and a half. We've discussed all kinds of possibilities. How do we know that when we leave this room, we'll both remember the same things? We have to write something; it's the only way we can be sure that we agree."

That's one of the most compelling arguments in favor of memoranda that I've ever heard. Not to mention that they help fend off the legal worries implied by film producer Samuel Goldwyn's famous quote, "A verbal agreement isn't worth the paper it's written on."

Although the process of reaching an agreement is sometimes complicated, writing a memo of that agreement should be kept simple. You don't need anything more complicated than a blank sheet of paper. The clearest format is the following modification of an old newspaper formula. Start with the date and time, and then list this sequence:

Who: Who is making the agreement? Who will be playing? Who will be paying?

What: What will be played, and how much of it? Are there any special requests to be honored, or any special prohibitions to be respected?

Where: What is the location of the event, and is it an indoor or outdoor setting?

When: What is the time of the event (including advance time for setting up, the number and lengths of breaks, and the ending time)?

How much: How much will be paid? How and when will it be provided—for example, will it come all at once or in installments? Do you need an advance of good-faith money?

Once those important parameters have been established, go on to more specific details. If you (or your group) have special needs, this is the opportunity to list them. Help nonmusicians know what is important to you—lighting requirements, chair requirements, protection from the elements if you are to play outdoors. This is also the place to list the client's special requirements. Will the dress be formal or casual? Is there a wedding ceremony whose musical pattern has to be outlined and planned?

If all this is beginning to sound complicated, rest assured that it doesn't have to be. Details always add up; that's what they do. But they fall into broad categories that you can organize ahead of time. With experience, you will come to recognize concerns that show up over and over again. You can use the above formula as a template for generating your own personal checklist.

Client copy (Retain for your records)

Your String Quartet

Performance Agreement

YSQ contact :________________________ Phone : ______________________

Address : ______________________

____

Client name:__________________________

We will perform at your:____

On: (date) ______________________Location:_______________________________
(Please include a map or adequate directions to the site when the contract is returned.)

Starting time:____________________ Ending time:____________________
(We will arrive 15 minutes in advance of the starting time to set up.)

♦ Please indicate whether you prefer us to wear *formal* (black dresses for women, and tuxedoes for men) or *casual* dress (dresses/skirts for women, and suits for men).
Formal__________Casual__________

♦ We require four chairs **without** arms. If we are to play outdoors, we **must** be in an area which is protected from the wind and **completely** shaded from the sun.
Will this be an indoor__________ **OR** an outdoor__________ event?

Our first hour of performance will be without a break. We will take a 10-minute break for each additional hour of playing.

In addition to works on our repertoire list, we can play specific music by arrangement. We must, however, have **at least** 2 weeks notice for any special requests. Please list necessary information for wedding ceremonies on a separate sheet. Be sure to include where in the ceremony the music is to take place, and for whom (e.g. bridal processional; bridesmaids' processional; seating of mothers; bridal recessional, etc.).

The total charge for your event is $__________. In order to reserve the date of performance, we must receive a 50% (non-refundable) deposit on this charge. The remaining balance is due at the completion of our performance. **Please make checks payable to the contact person listed above.**

Feel free to call us if you have any questions or wish to make further arrangements.

YSQ contact signature : ________________________ Date :______________

♦ *I have read and approved the above and am including a 50% deposit of $ ______________ with the return of this agreement.*

(Please sign and date) ____

Then you can go further. As your group works more and more, the agreement process can be aided by turning the checklist into a prepared form. A musician's earliest playing experiences are usually with friends and family, and in those relationships, complications can (ideally) be worked out smoothly as they occur. But as you start to deal with people you know less well, remember that the more you can prepare ahead of time, the better off everyone will be. This is where a contract form can facilitate negotiations. The pictured sample on the previous page shows how details can be organized into a helpful and businesslike contract. Keep it simple; one page is all you'll need (until you land your touring and recording contracts).

If demand grows and you find yourself playing often, you should give serious consideration to joining the musicians' union. Speaking as a longtime member and former steward, I believe there are many benefits to joining, including the availability of standard contract forms and established pay scales. Negotiations are easier when there is a base to work from.

Now that you know how to write agreements, remember the next step: keeping them. Be dependable. Do everything you can to plan ahead, to be prepared, and to be punctual. The virtuoso who shows up at the wrong place or on the wrong day is still a virtuoso, but he or she is not appreciated as much. And the contract has been broken.

Making—and writing—clear agreements is a simple but important act that improves the final musical experience. It helps everyone, employers and musicians alike. Once needs and expectations have been made clear, all the participants can go into the event with ease and confidence. Try it; everyone will like it.

The Fine Art of Faking 17

STARTING IN OUR EARLIEST YEARS, most string players are trained to learn and perform previously composed works with precision and thoroughness. From beginners' pieces to the classics—from "Twinkle, Twinkle" to a Bartók concerto—we diligently study the score (or listen to recorded examples), practice the notes, and strive to play our pieces both accurately and musically.

This is certainly a good way to work, and I'm all in favor of it; in fact, I love it. But at times, the demands of musical life strain the resources of our preparation. At times, we are suddenly asked to do unfamiliar or difficult playing in unfamiliar or difficult circumstances.

At those times, to do our best, we have to fake it.

In music, as in life, the ability to adjust and adapt in stressful situations has high survival value. It's unfortunate that we use the word "fake" to describe this important, multilevel skill. "Fake" sounds so . . . fake. Like a forgery, a falsehood. But it's really much more than that.

The truth is that what we call "faking" is close to the spontaneous, improvisatory wellsprings of music. Its many forms call on all of a player's musical knowledge, spirit, and instrumental ability. The musical skills that allow a player to join an unfamiliar situation and contribute to it come from the whole range of his or her musicianship. Coping with new music, playing by ear, keeping up with an ensemble, taking cues (both seen and heard) from other players and from the music, sight-reading music that's really too hard to sight-read—all of these situations, and more, give us opportunities to fake creatively.

This is not a comprehensive manual. Entire books could be written on the subject. But by offering examples taken from real-life music making, it will give a look at the kinds of situations in which good faking can save the moment. Knowing how and when to fake, recognizing when to do it—and when to lay out—is part of the skill.

Let's start with the field that I know best: classical music. This may seem an unlikely region to look to for our examples but, as we will see, there are treasures to be found.

The following instance from the world of chamber music shows many aspects of high-level faking. The Kolisch String Quartet became legendary for playing its large and varied repertoire by memory. But all the members of the group admitted that the real-life urgencies of touring and playing affected performance from day to day, and that they had to find ways of covering for fatigue and memory lapses.

In an interview for *Strings* Magazine ("Eugene Lehner at 84," March/April 1991), Kolisch Quartet violist Eugene Lehner revealed one of these methods. When asked if the quartet ever suffered memory slips, Lehner said, "There was hardly a performance without one; the question was only how serious. The only one to whom nothing ever happened was [second violinist Felix] Khuner. Once in Paris—we had traveled all night and were rather sleepy—we played the Beethoven Op. 95. You know the second theme of the second movement—the viola begins, and suddenly I realized, 'For God's sake, I have to start this and I don't know how it goes, and if I don't play, there is nobody.' And then I hear Khuner playing my part. Afterwards I said to him, 'How on earth did you know I wasn't going to play?' He said, 'You idiot, you were in fourth position on the D string.' I used to play it on the open A. With half an eye, he saw that I was somewhere else on the fingerboard. That quick reaction, it's just incredible. And you know, the other two were sitting right opposite and didn't notice anything."

A great example of great faking—at the highest level. The notes were right; only the instrumentation had changed.

Playing the classics of chamber music by heart is a rare practice and might not seem relevant to most musicians. But the cited moment offers compelling instruction in what a good ensemble player needs to do: know the music, listen to what's happening, watch what's happening, anticipate what's going to happen, and prioritize what's important (in order to play the viola solo, Khuner had to leave his own part out).

In the complex way that was typical of him, Khuner himself commented on this kind of happening with an insight that was also a joke. I once heard a colleague ask him, "Felix, how on earth is it possible to memorize the second violin part of a Haydn Quartet?"

"It's not possible. Absolutely not! I memorized the whole quartet and played what was missing."

"Wait a minute. 'Played what was missing'? If you did that, everyone else would have played already. You'd be late!"

"Ah no," Khuner said, raising an eyebrow. "Quick reflexes!"

The musical prioritizing that came so naturally to Khuner is a key aspect of alert faking. Orva Hoskinson of San Francisco, an experienced voice teacher and accompanist, states it clearly: "Some of these vocal accompaniments were written by composers who were much better pianists than I. When difficult passages show up, I give them three days of diligent practice. At the end of that time, if it's still not working, I start looking for what I can leave out without harming the effect."

Knowing what to leave out "without harming the effect" is an important part of doing justice to difficult or—let's face it—impossible music.

Yes, impossible. Composers in the throes of creation do not often stop to ask themselves if the middle voices can play all those notes at the indicated tempo. And conductors caught up in the excitement of performance often push a piece far beyond its indicated tempo, toward the impossible.

This was not generally true of the solid, steady-beating maestro Joseph Krips. Some years ago, in the theater parking lot after a San Francisco Symphony rehearsal with Krips, I was grabbed by my friend, colleague, and former teacher Harry Rumpler. "Young man," he counseled loudly as he squeezed my arm, "take advantage of this opportunity to play all the notes on the last page of *La Mer.* Most conductors try to do the whole page in one flick of the stick."

I did take advantage of that Kripsian opportunity. And through the years I learned the truth of what Rumpler said about most of the conducting fraternity: They took it fast. They take other things fast, too, which leads to another important faking guideline. When everyone else reaches the end and you're not finished, stop!

Richard Strauss' works are famous for the demands they make on instrumentalists; Strauss excerpts have been on every audition list I've ever seen. And sometimes his required tempos are already too fast to be pushed. In 1989, Christoph von Dohnányi conducted *Die Frau ohne Schatten* at the San Francisco Opera. The maestro combined his superb ear with a demanding, generally no-nonsense rehearsal style. During the first orchestra reading, we reached a very difficult passage and it sounded like breaking glass. Musicians shuffled and chuckled. "It is playable," said the maestro. "I just conducted it in Vienna. I have heard it played."

The rehearsal went on. We reached another hard passage. It sounded like splintering wood. "It is playable," said the maestro. "I have heard it."

The rehearsal went on. We reached a ghastly passage that sounded like an avalanche in the Swiss Alps. There was an embarrassed silence, and then the maestro said, to much relieved laughter, "Well, maybe that's not playable."

A carpool colleague—a violinist—and I compared our philosophies of how to traverse those difficult places. He said about one of them, "When the triplets are too fast, I will play the first two notes of each group of three. That will keep the right rhythm, every note I play will be correct in its place, and my accuracy will be .666, which is a pretty good average in baseball."

(I have to end this story properly, however. By performance time the orchestra sounded magnificent, as even the conductor acknowledged.)

These examples from classical music show some of the dimensions of faking. But usually when that word is used, popular and folk music come to mind. The famous line, "I don't know the song, but if you hum a few bars I'll play along with you" is part of our linguistic culture. The public assumes that musicians in general know how to do that, that it "just happens" for them.

Well, it does happen, but only after practice. No one is born knowing skills. Everyone has to learn them. And playing by ear is one of those skills.

I admit that some exceptional individuals do learn very quickly. The wonderfully versatile pianist Lincoln Mayorga told me many years ago that he had had to develop special techniques to learn to play pieces exactly as the composer had written them. "You know my ear. If I hear the chord sequence once, I can play something similar right away." This is the same man who was once asked how he could transpose difficult music so fluently when he accompanied singers. "I don't know," he replied. "My ear hears how it should sound and my fingers know where to go."

These abilities sound like magic, but they depend on many hours at the piano, where "the fingers" (read "the mind") learn where the notes are on the keyboard, and thus "where to go." The magic is always in such practice. And playing by ear can be practiced, just like everything else. By playing along with CDs, with the radio, with a television set (just imagine how many commercial jingles there are), one can get the feel of playing by ear without having to go public right away. Warming up by trying out contemporary popular tunes or standards is also a good approach.

Other knowledge about music also helps. The more you know, the better off you are. Dances are characterized by their rhythms; keep rhythmic integrity, and you're making a contribution. Songs tend toward distinctive patterns of repetition; recognize that structure, stay with it, and you're helping out. The more you know about other kinds of instruments—and their instrumentalists—the more you can foretell what's coming next just by watching other players move.

You can see this kind of listen-look-learn approach in action on Itzhak Perlman's video *In the Fiddler's House* (Angel/EMI Classics 77827). As he is joining in with practiced klezmer groups, Perlman's beautifully expressive face shows when he recognizes a tune, when he's puzzled by a harmony, when he perceives a structural pattern. Sometimes he even seems mildly embarrassed to be playing along without preparation, but he does it, and with bold musical momentum—also an instructive example.

It's important to recognize that what starts as faking doesn't have to stay that way. Perlman now tours the world with his well-learned program of Jewish music from Central Europe. It's the real thing.

But what about that situation we've all seen in the movies, where perfection is instant? Someone hums part of a tune, the pianist starts to play chords, the drummer adds a beat, the bassist adds a line, others join in, and in just a few minutes a big band is playing—impromptu, by ear, and flawlessly. This kind of scene is a vision of the finest faking possible.

Well, in this kind of scene the faking . . . has been faked! That big band was carefully rehearsed before filming. It sounds perfect because it was prepared to be perfect. Which is probably the best reminder for us to end with: Fake when you have to, but remember that it is always right to practice and be prepared.

18 Heimberg's Handy Hints: Tips and Tricks of the Trade

VIOLIST MICHAEL TREE HAS SAID, "Anything that improves the comfort of the musician improves the tone of the instrument." Playing a stringed instrument well—and comfortably—is a lifelong endeavor in which success can be measured in millimeters. Every little bit counts. That is why we string players are always seeking the most efficient fingering, the most gracefully appropriate bowing, the most productive way of practicing.

That is also why we put shoulder rests on our instruments and cushions on our chairs. Comfort can be sought everywhere the instrument touches the player and the player touches the world. It has to do with the whole musician and the whole environment of music making.

The basic source of true comfort is good body awareness and a well-practiced instrumental technique. That foundation can be supplemented, not replaced, by adjustments to one's instrument and surroundings. But once that foundation is in place (or under construction), there are many minor changes that can be made toward a freer enjoyment of playing.

I've been experimenting and adjusting for years, and not just with my instruments and the usual appurtenances (spare strings, shoulder pad, and so on). My viola case—like Batman's utility belt—also holds needle and thread, Velcro strips, cosmetic sponges, all-purpose rubber bands, scissors, surgical tubing, a length of bicycle inner tube, and more. I try things out. I putter. I tinker.

Here, then, are a few of my experimental results. I do not offer them as prescriptions, but as encouragements to make your own trials and adjustments. Doing so is part of our craft. It's part of the satisfaction, part of the comfort, and part of the fun.

Properly directing the bow is a little like being a parent; it requires a balance of firmness and permissiveness that takes years to learn. The contact points where our fingers touch the bow are among the most important places of our art. They are the transition areas between our intentions and our sound. The purposes of the mind, the weight of the arm, the subtleties of the fingers all focus at those spots. How we hold the bow influences everything else we do with the instrument.

I am very careful about how I describe holding the bow. I don't want the action to get burdened by heavy words. For example, I hate the expression *bow grip*—it sounds like something from the World Wrestling Federation. Instead, I think that words such as *cradle, carry,* or *cherish* give a better emotional sense of what bowing is like.

But sometimes, when there is a lot of playing to do, we have to cherish the bow for hours and hours at a time. At those times, a little bit of help can be . . . a big help. One type of help is found by sliding something over the bow stick to make it a little larger and easier to hold. Some of the bowing aids I've seen used in this way are three-inch lengths of surgical tubing, or the little rubber tubes sold in stationery stores as pencil grips, or small rubber plumbers' O-rings.

There's something else I use now: latex clerks' thimbles. You know, the rubber caps that you put over your thumb to help you turn pages of paper. I started trying this idea out when San Francisco Opera presented Wagner's *Ring* cycle one summer. It really worked well for me, especially when playing tremolo during the fifth hour of *Götterdammerung*. Just make a small hole in the thimble's tip (they come in several sizes—more room for experimenting), remove the frog from your bow, and slide the thimble on, with the large open end toward the tip of the bow. Work it on all the way up to the leather winding before replacing the frog. The result is a flexible bow helper whose stippled surface seems to be holding you as much as you're holding it. For added security, it is also possible to add small holes that allow your third finger and thumb to touch the wood of the stick.

Another place of magic is where the instrument touches the player's body. This is significant for all string players, but especially for violinists and violists, who support their instruments against gravity. Shoulder rests or pads are a great aid.

I remember that in my student days there were still older violinists who referred to shoulder pads as "crutches," an insulting term that implied that anyone who used them was physically unfit to play the violin. This characterization was usually made by short men with broad shoulders and no necks (men "built like a fire hydrant," as violinist Stuart Canin once put it), who seemed to be able to "plug in" their violins and simply play. That doesn't work for everyone. Adjusting a shoulder rest to suit the body of the player is an important part of the search for comfort. Like most violists, I tinker a lot with my shoulder rest. Violas come in all shapes and sizes, violists come in all shapes and sizes, and the shapes and sizes of commercial shoulder rests are just as varied—but not always in the right way. So we use all kinds of tools to adjust them: cosmetic sponges, rubber bands and chamois, Velcro and handkerchiefs.

But often we also need to protect the instrument from the shoulder rest, to help our psychological comfort. Although I admire the ergonomic concepts of several commercial brands, I am alarmed by their engineering. There's too much hardware dangerously close to the wood of the instrument; any metal near the wood should have a protective covering. Bare wires can be covered with tubing. Vinyl tubing is strong and effective for straight wires, while surgical tubing is easier to bend around corners. Electricians' tube shrink-wrap is aesthetically pleasing once you've taken the time and effort to apply it. These aids can also be used on nuts, bolts, and similar protuberances.

Lately, I have been using a simple device that covers the metal back of my shoulder rest: a piece of bicycle inner tube. Just get a used tube from the bicycle shop (they often will give them away), cut it to length, and slide it over the body of the shoulder rest, like a sleeve. It protects your instrument, provides a little extra padding, and sometimes even looks interesting.

Cellists may not need shoulder rests, but they have problems of their own. Ruth Lane, an elegantly tall cellist in the San Francisco Opera Orchestra, wanted to sit straight when she played. But she had to bend her head to the right to avoid getting poked in the side of the head by the tuning peg on her C string. The solution: remove the peg and replace it with a Posture Peg, a gearing mechanism tuned with a key. This adjustment works perfectly for her.

Here is another contribution to psychological comfort: taming the mute. All players need mutes, although we usually don't think much about them (unless they rattle, fall off in performance, or aren't there when the music says *con sordino*.) But they are worth thinking about. During the great San Francisco Symphony tour of Europe in 1973, I was touched by the ingenuity of our Soviet colleagues. They did not have access to high-quality manufactured mutes, but they had a practical alternative: money. They would tightly roll up a paper ruble note and thread it through the strings between the fingerboard and the bridge, where it could slide up and down as needed.

I thought that trick was an impoverished substitute for the real thing until 20 years later, when I saw some colleagues who had emigrated from the former Soviet Union. They were still using the same kind of technique, this time with dollars. I asked them about their money-mutes and got a compelling answer: "It does not fall off, it does not buzz, it works as mute, and it costs less than mute." Rolled-up bills are easy enough to get, so I tried it with dollar bills and liked it. (Just think: You can use francs for French music, lire for Italian, Deutschmarks for German—very subtle musical effects!) I've also tried thin strips of leather, or trim from old eyeglass cases, applied in the same way. With the right weight and firmness, the tone is sweet and the mute is silent when you slide it into place.

By the way, if you use a rubber mute and want to get rid of the creaky-squeaky sound it makes when you put it on or take it off the bridge in a hurry, try dripping a drop of candle paraffin into the slot and then wiping it off. According to violist Martin Andersen of the New Jersey Symphony, this provides just enough lubrication to eliminate the unwanted sound.

Going back to the theme of comfort, here is another important aid. In radio interviews, violinist Nadja Salerno-Sonnenberg once talked about having to "force calluses" after a layoff from playing. That's too bad. Forcing of any kind is not good for violin playing. There are other ways to firm up the left-hand fingertips—NuSkin, for example. This liquid bandage can be painted or sprayed onto the fingertip, and after just two minutes of drying, the liquid forms a malleable, protective cap for the finger. It can be played on immediately, while the finger reestablishes its own protective padding underneath. I've used the substance in a variety of circumstances: after layoffs, after washing in hot water, and even after cutting my finger in a kitchen accident. It worked well every time.

I'm sure every player has personal ideas for increasing creature comforts while playing—or for solving any of the little annoyances in a string player's life. Personally, I'm always looking for more. If you have ever discovered, devised, or daydreamed some helpful trick, share it with your friends and colleagues. Together, we musicians may someday compile an encyclopedia of crafty and useful gimmicks!

19 Lessening Audition Agonies

NOBODY LIKES AUDITIONS, but everyone has to play them. From the informal tryouts of student ensembles to the complex procedures of the major symphony orchestras, they are a difficult fact of every musician's life. They tell us what grade we will get, where we will sit, and—at the highest, hardest professional levels—whether or not we get the job.

It is easy enough to understand why professional auditions exist. After all, musicians are trained to be heard, and anyone who plans to hire a musician certainly deserves to hear that person play.

Auditions represent the most difficult playing one can be asked to do. Part competency test, part job interview, part bare-knuckle competition, auditions compress tension, desire, and extremely demanding music into just seven to 12 minutes of playing. And in those seven to 12 minutes, the people who are listening try to review and evaluate all of a candidate's prior decades of training and experience, with the goal of selecting "the best" player for the long-term job. The candidates run a sprint to qualify for a marathon. And for all but one, the result can mean disappointment, self-doubt, and more auditions in the future—if fatigue does not overcome ambition.

It is not surprising, then, that auditioning is usually considered a musical ordeal, not a musical joy. As Zaven Melikian, then concertmaster of the San Francisco Opera Orchestra, once aptly put it, "In recital, you play what you want to, the way you want to, and hope they like it. In an audition, you play what they tell you to, the way you think they want you to . . . and hope you're right!"

The key to playing a good audition is preparation. Of course, any musician considering a professional classical career needs to have a solid foundation. But good training, experience in ensemble playing, and a general education in music are just the start of audition preparation. Auditions are a special event, and they require special planning. A serious applicant should know in advance what is coming and should be ready for it. The modern American symphony audition has become formalized almost to the point of ritual. During the last three decades, conventions have been developed that are now used by almost every orchestra, with only minor variations from one to another. Knowing those conventions and preparing to face them is one of the auditioner's most urgent tasks.

A few of the most important conventions are open announcements, stipulated audition music, player anonymity, and selection participation by committees of orchestra members. Each can influence the auditioner's preparation and playing. And because the whole experience can also affect a player's state of mind, the emotional component of auditioning needs preparation, too.

Rumor networks spread information early, but the first official indication that an orchestra has an opening and is going to run an audition will come from the musician's union, the American Federation of Musicians. There will be an advertisement in the *International Musician,* the Federation's monthly newspaper, as well as a notice on the union's electronic bulletin board. Thirty years ago, only the major orchestras advertised openings in the *International Musician,* and then only occasionally. In those not-so-distant days, conductors could usually hear and hire whom they wanted to, when they wanted to. This could lead to abuses, favoritism and prejudice being the most common. (Readers of the biographies of Fritz Kreisler and Carl Flesch will remember that, early on, neither of those future greats could satisfy hidebound Joseph Hellmesberger, Sr., the influential player-teacher-conductor of the Viennese musical establishment.) Private auditions, limited invitational auditions, and job offers based on reputation—or friendship—were commonplace.

All that has changed, at least in the United States. As the principle of tenure has been established and as orchestra members have insisted on their right to be consulted in the hiring process, contractually defined audition procedures have become the standard of the profession—including, for orchestras of all levels, the requirement of a published announcement. The announcement means that the American Federation of Musicians has confirmed that an opening does exist, that an open search for a candidate is in progress, and that applicants are invited from all parts of the country—and from all over the world.

It also means competition. It is common for more than a hundred people to apply for each opening. Even though there are sometimes local favorites for a particular position, victory is never certain. No one can be sure of being tops on any given day, and personal confidence should be based on a sense of self-worth, not an expectation of victory. It can be extremely painful to expect to win, and then to lose. It is very healthy to expect to play well because you're ready, and let the outcome take care of itself.

I have often told students and audition consultees, "Your work is to practice well and play well, not to predict. You never know when you'll find yourself going against a champion. And she never knows when she'll find herself going against you!" (Of course, this attitude is often easier to espouse than to have.)

Many professional orchestras now stipulate the solo pieces to be played in their auditions, and almost all of them publish lists of required orchestra excerpts. This is meant to set a standard of professional requirements and to create a common frame of reference for comparison between applicants. The idea is that if everyone has worked up exactly the same pieces, it will be easier to determine who has done the best job of preparation.

Sometimes these long and detailed lists are also meant to do more: They discourage the inexperienced and the fainthearted. Candidates who decide not to audition because they "can't learn all that in two months!" are right. They're not supposed to learn it all in two months. Audition practice should begin not months but years before the audition.

Stipulated solo pieces are usually classics of the literature, familiar friends to get reacquainted with rather than to meet for the first time. Often, because of time limitations, only the first movement of a concerto is required—and almost as often, only the first page is heard. It would be a serious mistake to become a one-page player, though. Some years ago, a cellist performing Tchaikovsky's *Rococo Variations* for an audition at which the solo was not stipulated started out very well but proved to be completely unprepared for the later variations when the committee asked him to jump ahead. That kind of haphazard preparation is just what orchestras are not looking for.

In fact, study of orchestra excerpts should be incorporated into the practice of any serious musician as soon as he or she expresses an interest in becoming a professional. Excerpts are worth the study; one hour spent with the Scherzo from Mendelssohn's *A Midsummer Night's Dream* will do as much for a violinist's spiccato as anything else in the literature. (Brass and woodwind players know the importance of orchestral material; it is a mainstay of their repertoire and training.)

Lists of requirements make it much easier for the prospective candidate to focus the work of preparation. Gone are the painful hours of planning strategy: "What's my best piece? Can I ask them to stop me before the cadenza?" Gone, too, is the frightening specter of sight-reading, at least until the very late finals. When a published list is 20 pieces long, it is unlikely that anything else will be asked until the field has been culled to a very few candidates.

An auditioner should not count on this, however. The ability to sight-read music is a reasonable demand in the classical field. Gerhard

Samuel used to include sight-reading in every audition for the Oakland Symphony in the 1960s and '70s. He once explained the philosophy behind this practice: "The audition needs to have music from major works, which anyone who is serious about getting the job should already know. Then there need to be two pieces of sight-reading. One should be readable, and the candidate should be able to read it. The other should be something that nobody can read at sight—so you have a chance to watch him work it out."

A few years ago, a joke was current in orchestra circles that combining player anonymity with very specific lists might lead to the hiring of a gifted Suzuki student who couldn't read music at all. The joke is an exaggeration, but not by much. I was once present at an audition for the San Francisco Symphony in which a finalist was asked to play an excerpt and then to continue playing beyond it. (Yes, it is fair to ask that.) The bracketed 24 bars were excellent—as his playing had been through the whole process. The next eight were a disaster, and he lost the audition to a player who had either studied the whole piece or was simply a better reader.

As long as orchestras retain their current form, learning the canon of the repertoire will be one of the instrumentalist's important responsibilities. We have come quite a distance from the days of "expect to play anything" to "learn 16 bars of this and 32 of that"—but we can always go back again. A recent Chicago Symphony audition for a titled cello chair required applicants to know "cello solos from the repertoire."

In recent years, the screen has become another familiar fixture at orchestra auditions. Most orchestras use it during their preliminaries, and a few use it throughout the process. The Metropolitan Opera Orchestra has held fully screened auditions for years, to good effect.

The use of the screen maintains anonymity and thus prevents discrimination based on race, age, sex, or favoritism. These are worthy objectives, and during screened auditions special precautions are taken to keep any identifying information from getting to the listeners. Candidates are asked not to talk, not to warm up in the same room, not to make unusual sounds or noodle on their instruments. Musicians with unusual shoes—such as high heels or clogs—may be asked to remove them before entering the room.

One result of these high-minded efforts is that candidates' nerves can be affected even more than usual. Some find the whole situation unnatural and strange, and it is. They find it hard to project their playing to an audience they can't see, an audience they imagine might not even be there. They get rattled—and they are not relieved when they learn that there are other candidates who relax because they prefer not to look their listeners in the eye. Again, special preparation is in order.

Candidates would do well to practice in the presence of a screen, and to play screened auditions for their friends in order to get used to this artificial situation as much as possible.

Nerves are a natural part of any stressful situation. Held within a normal range, they are a healthy vital sign. But it often takes special practice to hold them in that range. Auditions are an especially intense experience, and they are over so quickly that it's not always possible to "play yourself in."

I once played an in-orchestra audition for colleagues whom I knew very well, just two weeks after having been the target of an attempted mugging. (I had been very lucky; the muggers were scared away by passersby.) The audition was hospitable and genial, and nothing terrible happened. But I can swear that I felt more nerves while auditioning than while being mugged.

Of course, the people on the other side of the audition screen are not criminals out to get you (no matter how you feel about them). They are a committee of experienced, knowledgeable orchestra members who take their job seriously. All of them are pleased by fine playing. All of them want to select a good colleague for their orchestra and want to pass a likely candidate to the finals. All of them want to be fair and try to put a candidate at ease when an audition is uneven or marginal. (The committee can talk to the candidate, even though the candidate can't talk back.) However, the eye can be more forgiving than the ear, and hearing auditions behind a screen throws every glitch and scratch into sharp relief.

Auditions are tough even without a screen, of course. On one occasion in the early 1980s, the formidable Kurt Herbert Adler of the San Francisco Opera was hearing unscreened cello auditions. One excellent cellist began his audition superbly but weakened as the hearing went on—so much so that what began as a winning chance ended up sounding very unpromising. After the player left the room, he mentioned to the personnel manager that his child had been sick the night before. "She was crying all night. I couldn't get any sleep," he said. "I guess it caught up with me." The manager immediately went back into the audition room and told Adler about that mitigating circumstance. Adler, whose first allegiance was always to the standards of the San Francisco Opera, replied, "Sir, there is no guarantee that the child will not get sick during the opera season. We will continue looking."

The profession of orchestra playing is beautiful to be in, but very hard to enter. This brief tour of orchestra auditions is not meant to make them any more likeable, but I hope it is has made them a bit more understandable. Once the hurdle has been leaped, it turns out to have been only the start of the real work of lifelong playing and learning.

PART THREE

VIEWS FROM THE MUSICAL LIFE

There are many levels—and joys—in the musical life: playing, working with others, belonging to a musical community, belonging to musical history. It's much more than just good sound.

Gerhard Samuel, the conductor who hired me as a violist in the Oakland Symphony, had a programming philosophy that was very popular with contemporary composers. He told me once how he configured the programs. "On a symphony program," he said, "give them something old that they might know or might not, but they don't object to listening to: Vivaldi, Bach. Then give them a name soloist, somebody they want to come hear." (And we had some real name soloists: pianists Leon Fleisher and Glenn Gould, violinists Ruggiero Ricci and Christian Ferras. . . .)

"Then," he said, "give them a big piece that they've heard before and want to hear again: a Brahms symphony, a Beethoven symphony.

"And when you've got them in with those three things, play something for them that they'd never turn around to listen to otherwise."

It's a fine formula for planning a program. It's also a good formula for making a life as a musician (especially if you'll allow me to take a few liberties in the comparison). Play the warhorses that you don't object to, and play the melodies that you would love to hear every night. Play with the best musicians you know—whether "best" means the best-known, the most talented, or simply the most fun. Embrace the works you're sight-reading as well as the pieces you know by heart, and welcome the colleagues you've never sat down to perform with before as well as the old friends who know your every technical pitfall. If you take on all the challenges and variety that a life in music can offer, then you will always find something—some musical challenge, some emotion freshly put into sound, or some new friend—that you never would have found otherwise.

An Orchestra Is Split

20

ON THE WEEKEND AFTER LABOR DAY, in 1979, San Francisco's musical year was about to begin as it had for decades, with the gala opening of the Opera season. But big things were afoot for music in San Francisco. The changes were to be momentous, more so than anyone realized at the time. It seemed a normal season opening: the opening nights of each production, the opening night parties, Opera in the Park, lines of people around the block waiting to buy standing-room tickets. The War Memorial Opera House hummed and sang with the sounds of round-the-clock work. Opera was in the air.

But the great transformation was also in the air and, in fact, under way. Across Grove Street, just south of the Opera House, an entire city block had been dug up. A large parking lot on land that had previously served as Commerce High School's athletic field was now a deep hole filled with a concrete foundation and an exposed infrastructure of pipes and wires. Louise M. Davies Symphony Hall, the new home of the San Francisco Symphony, was under construction.

Due to open the following September, ready or not (and it was not), Davies Hall would free the Symphony to perform or rehearse its expanding season on the same dates as the Opera—which would necessitate the founding of an entirely new Opera orchestra. This was to be probably the most significant major orchestra expansion in the United States since the formation of the NBC Symphony in 1937.

Although the San Francisco Opera and the San Francisco Symphony had long been separate organizations, for nearly half a century they had shared the use of the War Memorial Opera House. They had also shared many musicians. In 1979, 35 players did double service as members of the Opera and the Symphony. Suddenly, it was necessary to find, select, and hire dozens of new instrumentalists, some for the Opera Orchestra itself; others for the Symphony, to replace those who had gone across the street to the Opera.

Finding and selecting those musicians from hundreds of applicants was urgent and productive work that took the better part of a year. As orchestra manager for the San Francisco Opera at that time, I was close to the whole process.

The change would force musicians to make a difficult choice. Through the years, instrumentalists performing for both groups had filled their working time with a rich range of repertoire. Symphony or Opera? Each alone was very good; playing both had been wonderful. "I loved the variety," trumpeter Edward Haug once said. "After three months out of sight in the pit, it usually took me a couple of weeks to get used to being looked at by the audience when I was onstage with the Symphony, but I loved doing all that different music."

Of course the choice would not only be musical; it would also be professional. There were practical matters to hammer out. The Symphony's contract was already set; but the Opera management (led by General Director Kurt Herbert Adler) and the Musicians Union were in negotiations, trying to reach a new contract that would craft the future.

Preliminary auditions to select possible finalists began during this time, but the procedures and prospects had to be carefully described to the candidates. Openings were probable, but not certain. The company's exact needs would be known only when musicians had made their decisions, and that would be possible only after a contract was agreed upon.

The built-in uncertainties of this job description may have helped narrow the number of auditioners to something nearing manageable proportions, but just barely. Applicants still came out in numbers. Good jobs are a rare and precious commodity for classical musicians. When there is a chance to try for one, it has to be taken.

Good and suitable musicians are also precious. Listening to 30 to 40 players on an audition day was a little bit like panning for gold. Playing in an opera orchestra requires very special qualities. Most American instrumentalists are trained in the solo repertoire for their instruments, but not in the literature and musical traditions of opera. Vocal drama is a different kind of music from symphonic works, even though both are written in the same notation. It takes special skill and experience to respond correctly when a tenor holds a high note longer than usual, or when a chord has to be stretched to accommodate some action on the stage. Josef Gingold, the great concertmaster and teacher, once summed up the challenges concisely in his friendly, gravelly voice, saying, "I know how it is, my dear, I have been around a long time. In the Symphony you have four rehearsals for each program, and every performance is supposed to be the same. In the Opera you never have enough rehearsal, and every performance is different!"

All this was uppermost in the minds of the team of Opera representatives who heard the preliminary auditions. David Agler, then resident conductor, listened, watched, was interested in hearing what his fellow listeners observed, and was especially alert to how candidates related to the committee in conversation. Zaven Melikian, the orchestra's genial concertmaster, brought to bear his long experience and knowledge. He was perceptive about all instrumentalists—winds, brass, and strings—but he had a special interest in violinists. (The orchestra would need ten new ones.) When he thought there was time for him to work with a candidate, his examination could start to resemble a coaching session. This was fine until the lengthened session started to threaten the whole day's schedule. "Come on, Zaven," I said once, after a candidate had left, "another audition like that and you can give up the idea of eating lunch or dinner!"

Other principal players and members of the musical staff attended auditions as needed. Charles Siani, principal bassist, always brought a clear minded practicality when he listened. After one audition someone said, "That last player was a little unsteady rhythmically, but what a big, beautiful tone he had!" Siani answered, "There's nothing worse than a bad player with a big tone"—and that was that.

As orchestra manager, I not only organized the auditions, I was also part of the judging committee and attended all the sessions. It was exciting and gratifying to work for Adler in that capacity, because he did not think of the position of orchestra manager as simply bureaucratic. He considered it to be one of musical responsibility, part of the artistic staff. (Of course, there were many who said that working for Kurt Herbert Adler in any capacity was too exciting for them to touch. But that is a different story.)

The finals would be held with Adler in attendance. As general director and music director, he had responsibility for the final selection. But he trusted his staff, and the variety of listeners involved during the winnowing preliminaries probably helped find musicians with the necessary flexibility.

After four months of negotiation, the Opera and the Musicians Union reached agreement on a new contract, and the dual-service musicians could make their choices. The Symphony offered the security of a 52-week work year, and most players opted for that. Twelve musicians (including some of the Bay Area's better-known performers) chose to stay with the Opera. It became clear that the Symphony would have 12 openings in its 100-player roster—a sizable percentage, but manageable. The Opera, on the other hand, faced a real challenge: 26 of the new orchestra's 67 chairs had to be filled—nearly 40 percent.

We heard auditions at home and elsewhere. We used the Opera House in San Francisco, and we traveled. We listened in an old, little-used theater in Los Angeles, in college classrooms in Chicago, at the Manhattan School of Music in New York. We used hotel banquet rooms and theater rehearsal rooms. On one occasion, the room available for a trumpet audition was so small that the player was asked to turn around and play out the open window.

Hundreds of resumés arrived in the mail, dozens of phone calls came in every day. I was glad to answer questions by phone, but applications had to be in writing. Personal computers were only a rumor then, and the written applications were our way of keeping track of things. I would show up at auditions with two suitcases full of resumés, sorted and filed by instrument, city, and audition date and time—a 50-pound database. It was a heavy and primitive technique, but we never lost a candidate.

When I think of the rush and welter of that hectic year, some of those auditions jump up in memory. I recall the scholarly, elegant violin playing of the quiet, intense Adolf Bruk, a former Bolshoi concertmaster who had managed to get out of the Soviet Union and arrive in San Francisco at just the right time. "This man is clearly very fine," Adler whispered to me during the finals. Bruk was hired as the Orchestra's associate concertmaster, a post he held for 14 years until his retirement.

I also remember the whirlwind audition of the quick-moving, red-headed cellist Samuel Cristler, in New York. Cristler came up to me in the hallway and asked if he could play soon. "I'm performing the Haydn Concerto with the Rochester Philharmonic tonight, and the last train that will get me there on time leaves Grand Central Station in 18 minutes."

I was flabbergasted: "Are you sure you want to play now? You could come tomorrow."

"I have other commitments tomorrow. There's plenty of time, if I can just play now."

We let Cristler move up in sequence, and in the course of the next 13 minutes he played part of his concerto. ("This is what I'm performing tonight. I might take some of the tempos faster than usual because of the train schedule.") He also read some orchestra excerpts, played the piano (on which he was also a skilled performer), and asked about the possibilities of doing some conducting. (Agler replied, "You're talking to one of the Opera company's conductors; I think those posts are filled.")

He left with four minutes to catch his train. "I hope you make it," I said.

"No problem," he answered. "The cabs are good."

Months later, at the final auditions, I learned that he had been right. He had made the train and played his concerto. And he passed our finals and joined the Opera.

All auditions are interesting, and touching. When people with decades of training strive to demonstrate their skill under pressured and hurried conditions, the knowing listener has to be sympathetic even while being critical. Our candidates had run a prolonged gauntlet of preliminaries and finals; those who were offered employment had really accomplished something. And those of us working on the search had accomplished something, too. At least we thought so—we had formed a new Opera Orchestra, but no one knew what it would sound like!

On August 11, 1980, we would hear the new orchestra for the first time. The Opera House was not available for those first rehearsals, so the orchestra was set up on the stage of Herbst Theatre, in the Veterans' Building. This was a securable area, and Adler, always protective of the company's reputation, gave orders that the doors were to be locked and only trusted Opera personnel allowed to listen.

The long-awaited moment finally arrived. The stage was crowded with musicians and Opera staff members who wanted to be in on this new beginning. After some words of welcome, a final shuffling of chairs, and tuning, David Agler's downbeat came and the orchestra played. And it sounded wonderful! The blend of experienced players and new members worked well right from the start. It was a moment of great satisfaction—and relief—for everyone there.

Later, after that long rehearsal day, I was in Adler's office, talking over some other business. Near the end of our meeting, I decided to fish for a compliment. "I thought our orchestra sounded pretty good today, Mr. Adler." I waited for him to answer. Kurt Herbert Adler, by temperament and style, tended to shout his criticism and whisper his praise. He looked down at his desk, curled his lower lip and softly said, "Not bad."

That was high praise, but now I was greedy for more. "Tomorrow when we rehearse, is it OK if I leave the doors unlocked?" He looked up at me over the top of his glasses, managing a quarter smile, and said, still softly, "OK."

The San Francisco Opera Orchestra has received many superb reviews during the years since then, but that one lives in my memory.

21 Letter from the Pit

I LOVE MY WORK—which is a very good thing, because there are times of the year when I do an awful lot of it.

When the San Francisco Opera swings into full production, my viola and I will be spending many hours a week together in the Opera House pit. These days, in a tightly packed fall season of just three and a half months, the San Francisco Opera—one of the world's best—presents 70 performances of nine different operas, as much as some European houses do in a year.

It is a remarkable achievement, and it requires a remarkable intensity of work. Every department is in overdrive (*Crescendo! Accelerando!*). From early morning to late at night, the workshops, dressing rooms, and hallways of the Opera House reverberate with the sounds of stagehands hammering, costume racks rolling, singers singing (or warming up—not always a pretty sound), and people talking in half a dozen languages, all of which have a word for *tired*.

The building also reverberates with the sound of the orchestra. Whenever we play, that rehearsal or performance is broadcast over the Opera House speaker system. This happens often, since the orchestra puts in many double-service days, with rehearsals in the late morning and early afternoon and performances at night. Opera is very much larger than life; so is opera scheduling. Sometimes the orchestra works 11 and 12 services a week—and opera services are the longest in classical music.

One year when the touring Guarneri String Quartet passed through the Bay Area, violinist Arnold Steinhardt came to the Opera on one of the ensemble's rare nights off. The overture to Rossini's *Otello* has several instrumental solos, and he liked them all. Something else also impressed him. "You know, I play pretty demanding music, but it's usually only for an hour and a quarter or an hour and a half in an evening," he said. "To sit there playing well for a three-and-a-half hour performance, the way you guys do, is really an achievement."

Yes, we get to play great music—hour after hour, day after day. The work is satisfying, the amount of it ridiculous. But demanding as our modern schedule is, it contains many hard-won improvements since those days a few decades ago when the orchestra would work three months straight without a day off. We do now have our official weekly "43-hour free period" and some relief leave.

Even so, the effort is noticeable. In midseason there is an especially busy stretch when three shows are in production and three are in rehearsal. The administration calls this time "the stack of six." Orchestra members are more straightforward. We call it "the crunch."

And it really can crunch. There is a constant danger of injuries from overwork. Close to performance time, a walk through the hallways near the pit can sometimes seem like a visit to a living catalog of alternative medicines: heat before playing, ice after playing, stretches against walls and doors, tai chi, the Feldenkrais Method, the Alexander Technique—all the major and minor bodywork systems have been used by colleagues at one time or another to make playing easier and more informed.

Another way to make playing easier is to adjust one's instrument. My own recent experiment has been to shorten the playing length of the strings on my Raffaele Fiorini viola (which measures 16¾ inches) by having a specially cut ebony nut inserted into the fingerboard near the pegbox, but about half an inch away from where the nut usually goes. My decision was based on clear thinking, though not rigorous science—if I save 1⁄64 of an inch on every interval, by the end of the season I should be miles ahead.

Any change on an instrument's setup is an intrepid move for a violist. Among string players, bassists are the boldest about experimenting with the ergonomics of their instruments. Throughout history they have changed tunings, altered string-playing lengths, adjusted bridge angles, added extensions. The rest of us tend to be more conservative. We think of ourselves as the guardians of instrumental works of art passed down through time—which we are. The downside is that we often arrange ourselves to fit the instrument, even when it hurts.

So far the smallest adjustment to my Fiorini has yielded enormous results. Tone has not been affected, but ease of playing has. Intervals are a little bit closer together, which lightens the work of the left hand, and the strings speak more easily. The next time the Opera does *The Ring,* I won't have to shift to a smaller instrument in self-defense as I did the last time.

This year [1995] is the second season for our new concertmaster, Kay Stern. The story of how she became concertmaster has already begun to acquire a well-deserved, legendary glow as I've heard it retold by musicians around the country. A busy and respected violinist in New York, Kay served as concertmaster for the Cabrillo Festival in Santa Cruz in the summer of 1992. She had gone there for the music, and while there she met her future husband, who works as stage manager for the Festival every year. That's when she began to think about living on the West Coast.

Often the personal side of career decisions does not make it into the history books. Kay recalls a moment in a Santa Cruz coffee shop when she hesitated about ordering because she wasn't sure if she would like the way they made cappuccino. The counterman said, "Here, I'll make one for you. If you don't like it, you don't have to pay." And Kay thought, "I've got to live in California—this would never happen in New York!" Careers are built on insights like this.

Kay's story stands out even in the world of stories that is opera. Working in opera production is like living in an opera about producing operas. For every tale that is sung on stage at night, a thousand have been lived during the day. The outside world—sometimes called "real"—can start to seem quite slow-moving by comparison. Opera is compelling; it makes you watch and listen.

Of course, what you get to see from the pit depends a lot on where you sit. The orchestra is always lower than the stage, but musicians seated near the audience side have a good angle for seeing some stage depth. Those seated under the stage floor—which sometimes juts out over the pit—usually don't get to see anything. This might help their concentration. For those with reasonable sight lines, the temptation to watch the stage is constant—and dangerous. A musician's first responsibility, of course, is to make the right entrances and play the right notes.

The last two minutes of staging for *The Fiery Angel,* in the fall of 1994, offered plenty of distractions. This early opera by Prokofiev is a medieval tale of demonic possession and sexual hysteria, whose final stage directions call for a group of nuns to disrobe and be possessed by demons. Confronted with these unusual directions, the women of the chorus refused to comply. They quite rightly pointed out that public nudity was not part of their original job description. In the face of this personnel crisis, the Opera management showed great resourcefulness: They sought the services of experts, hiring exotic dancers from the famous Mitchell Brothers' O'Farrell Theater—women who disrobe in front of audiences nightly.

Talk about theatrical values! I have seldom felt so motivated to memorize music as I was for those last two pages of *The Fiery Angel.* Half-turned in my chair to look over my right shoulder, my viola scroll aimed at the conductor and my eyes aimed at the stage, I could see some of the events that took place near the proscenium and was grateful that they had been staged within my sight lines.

Now, it's true that colleagues seated near the far wall of the pit could see more, more easily. But colleagues seated under the stage could see almost nothing. I say "almost" because the bassoon section did report that every evening, at exactly the same place in the music, one lone naked female leg would hang over the edge of the stage above their heads. Those of us with better views told them about the rest. We tell everyone.

(Arnold Steinhardt's response to this tale was pointed: "Stories like this never happen in the world of chamber music!")

I've said that musicians placed under the stage don't get to see the operas, but they certainly get to hear them. Yes, there are singers on stage. And although all of us in the profession agree that opera without singers would be less complicated, we also admit that it would be less interesting. These remarkable musicians, whose bodies are their instruments, whose musical selves must be expressed and revealed each time they sing (or they are not really singing), live to a standard of musical involvement that is inspiring, that gives the form its meaning. We are grateful to them for fascinating the public.

And we are grateful to the public for being fascinated, and for so miraculously filling the Opera House night after night. No matter where we sit in the pit, we sometimes let our gaze go beyond the conductor, out into the theater. We watch the audience watch the stage.

The San Francisco Bay Area is blessed with a public that appreciates live performance, that supports three major orchestras in a two-block radius (Opera, Symphony, and Ballet), that knows and respects the dangers and achievements of what we do. I want those people to know that we appreciate them, and that we know they are there.

And that's the news from the pit.

22 The Freeway Philharmonic

ONE OF THE SAN FRANCISCO BAY Area's great musical treasures is its freelance pool of classical musicians. Skilled, devoted, and often overworked, this group of some 400 instrumentalists provides the musical core of many of our region's performing ensembles. From Santa Rosa to Santa Cruz, from Modesto to Monterey, freelancers do the playing—and the driving—that brings symphonic and chamber music to the loyal audiences around us.

They are the itinerant musicians of our time and place. They are the Freeway Philharmonic.

And they are good. Just listen to them. Just read the reviews of the Santa Rosa Symphony, or the Marin Symphony, or the Berkeley Symphony (a few of the groups that often share players). The Bay Area musicians in these orchestras have a depth of musical culture that responds vigorously whenever an interesting program and a dynamic conductor provide opportunity and focus.

It's no surprise that they can do this. The love of music is what brings people into this profession and helps keep them there. Meredith Brown, a French horn player who performs with the Marin Symphony, the Diablo Ballet, Western Opera Theater, and perhaps half a dozen other local organizations ("Yes, I am definitely a card-carrying member of the Freeway Philharmonic"), has expressed the musical satisfactions of her peripatetic professional life clearly and enthusiastically. "When I play with people I like," she explains, "when I show up at a job and there are people there I can communicate with without talking, and they dig my playing and I dig theirs, it's all worth it."

Classical musicians begin their studies very young. By the time they are ready to play professionally, most have studied and practiced their instruments for some 20 years. But it takes more than just good playing to secure a niche in the freelance world. There must be the ability to cope with the four M's of freelancing (Music, Miles, and Minimal Money). And players have to combine ability with dependability.

They have to be able to show up—at the right place, at the right time, ready to play—consistently, no matter how complicated the schedule gets.

It does get complicated. The San Francisco Musicians Union (AFM Local Six) maintains and makes available a master calendar of symphonic groups, showing the rehearsal and concert dates (and the conflicts!) of 17 different organizations that have union contracts. And 17 is not the limit of performing local ensembles.

No one can belong to all of these groups at one time, but many musicians belong to several of them. That kind of potential busyness makes a top priority of having a good date book, one with enough room to schedule in private teaching and extra gigs.

Freelancers organize their calendars or they stop getting called. But that organization does not always carry over into private life. Martha Rubin (flute and viola) tells the story of the day that she and her husband Nate (a distinguished Bay Area violinist, and the concertmaster of the Oakland Symphony for more than 30 years) had breakfast together in their Moraga home, chatted, cleared the table, and got into their separate cars to go to work. An hour and a half of driving time later, they were surprised to meet again—at work, in Santa Clara! They had kept their date books well; they just hadn't compared them. Yes, it takes planning—as well as talent, training, and a good set of wheels—to do this kind of work. Making a career of it calls for special versatility and energy.

Diana Dorman, a popular and respected clarinetist in San Francisco, gives a glimpse of what her career path demands: "I play principal clarinet for Lamplighters Music Theatre and Pocket Opera, and I am also the contractor for those groups. Also I'm the principal clarinet for the Berkeley Symphony, the second clarinet with the Western Opera Theater Orchestra, a sub and extra with San Francisco Opera, and I sometimes play with the Women's Philharmonic. Oh yes, I am also the music librarian for Lamplighters. And then there's my union work, too. . . . It all keeps me busy, but it's pretty localized. I don't put on the kind of miles that some of my colleagues do."

Like bassist Alex Glickman, who has been known to drive some 150 miles (one way) to Chico, or 200 miles to Redding, to play symphony concerts. (The thousands of miles he traveled to get here from Moscow don't count.) Or Tom Nugent, who played principal oboe in the Sacramento Philharmonic while continuing to teach more than 100 miles away at the University of California at Santa Cruz, as well as at the University of the Pacific in Stockton (only about 50 miles away). Nugent wholeheartedly backs the principle of always filling your gas tank in the evening—no matter how tired you are—because you never know what might delay you in the morning.

Of course, carpooling is a popular and economical way to share the driving load. "I like to carpool whenever I can," says Meredith Brown, "and I usually offer to drive, because I find that driving helps keep me focused. There is an awful lot of coming home late at night after concerts." Many orchestra managements now issue concert rosters and phone lists, which does help the carpooling. But sometimes there's no way around it: Getting to work just has to be a long, solitary drive.

Rufus Olivier was a freelancer early in his career, before becoming well-established as the distinguished and beloved principal bassoonist of both the San Francisco Opera and San Francisco Ballet Orchestras. He recalls his student years in Southern California: "I used to go play in the Kern County Symphony from South Central LA. I would talk my sputtering old car over the mountain pass: 'We can do it, baby. We can make it.' And I'd be thinking, 'There is no lane on this freeway meant for a car this slow—not one lane!'"

Yes, a reasonably good car is an important tool of this trade. Along with an instrument, of course. And that date book. And at least a good answering machine—plus maybe a pager and a cell phone. Being reachable and responsive, as well as being a good performer, keeps the calls coming in.

Music, miles, and minimal money. Much is demanded of these musicians, but not much is paid to them. The payments offered by the regional, metropolitan, and community organizations are far less than those offered by the major orchestras. Those majors—our own San Francisco Ballet, Opera, and Symphony—are the most prominent ensembles in the local musical landscape. They offer their members security and benefits: tenure, guaranteed annual income, health plans, paid vacations, instrument insurance. Because positions in them are so desirable, these orchestras are hard to join. Openings are infrequent, competitive auditions are open to the world, and there are always at least a hundred applicants for each available position.

It's true, though, that not all musicians want to join those echelons. Some have already been there—like Virginia Baker, the splendid former assistant concertmaster of the San Francisco Symphony, who joined the Berkeley Symphony in her retirement "to keep my hand in." Others have declared their preference for playing in small ensembles with exploratory repertoire.

But others make freelancing a full career. Violinist Ellen Pesavento has frequently played as a substitute and extra for the San Francisco Symphony and Opera. She is also the personnel manager for the California Symphony and the Sun Valley Festival, has a large class of students, and coaches chamber music at a private school in San Francisco. "I love the work, but it can be tiring. If you let it happen, you can kill yourself going for more and more money. Younger musicians won't tell you that, because they're building their careers. When you've done it for awhile, you see the importance of taking time off to get refreshed."

When the needs of young children or dependent parents cause players to push to the extreme, career success begins to look like overwork. "What need of a trout if there be troutlets enough?" asked Sancho Panza—but he wasn't driving all over Northern California to do his fishing.

The musical rewards of the Freeway Philharmonic can be rich, the financial rewards more modest. But the musicians who participate in this way of life offer musical experience to the Bay Area that enriches us all. And though life on the musical highway can be demanding, there is a further aspect to it that Rufus Olivier has pointed out: "If you are a musician, and you are making your living as a musician, you are a success!"

23 Marking the Music

EVERY MUSICIAN I KNOW BRINGS a pencil to rehearsal—or at least borrows one. Sharp, soft lead and a good eraser are among our most important tools. We all mark our music. And we've been marking it for years: at our teacher's studio, in our practice rooms, on the bus, in rehearsal. Marking the music—clearly, correctly, completely—is an important craft. It helps learning, helps interpretation, and helps performance. Also, as we will see, it can be a welcome distraction during long talks by the conductor.

Marking well is an act of generosity. We do not mark music only for ourselves, but also for our students, for our stand-partners, for the sub who might have to read a performance on 20 minutes' notice, for the different person we will be ten years from now—the person who might not remember that clever fingering we were so lucky to discover.

Right from the beginning, we have to recognize the difference between marking the music and marking it up.

"I don't really mind comments in the music when they're apt and witty (though it's hard to legislate wit)," Laure Campbell, the librarian of the San Francisco Opera Orchestra, once told me. "But scribbling is a no-no! For instance, if you have a big cut that's hard to see, don't try to bury it in pencil lead; cover it with a piece of white paper cut to size. There are also transparent tapes that can be removed later without hurting the paper. Use them."

Emergency subs at San Francisco Opera have sometimes thanked me for marking my music so clearly. Well-placed musical warnings saved them from falling into traps.

The beginning of the music does not always coincide with the top of the first page. Maybe excerpts are to be played for an in-school demonstration, or maybe only two arias are going to be showcased out of an entire opera. Whatever the reason for starting in the middle of any work, the word *START* should be written at the very beginning of the printed material, with an arrow or written directions indicating the new beginning place. The upper left-hand corner is where musicians always look first, so that is where they should get their first directions. It does no good to bury the word *START* on page 45 if there is no way for the player to know about it 44 pages earlier. But "START on page 45 and rehearsal letter M" written at the top of page 1 will tell the whole story—and will avoid the potential catastrophe of the orchestra's starting at several different places at once.

The symbols for down bow (⊓) and up bow (V) are probably the first ones we encounter in our studies, and they are with us for our entire lives.

These marks should be used *one at a time*. When used together, they produce this confusing symbol: ⊓V, which often shows up in music, but shouldn't. The rule is simple: Erase the old mark before applying the new one! (If you're rushed in a rehearsal and have to make a change quickly, then take time later to clean up the part.)

Printed music is rich in information, but it still does not tell us everything we need to know before we begin. For example, the time signature might be 4/4, but how is the conductor going to beat it? In four? In two? In eight?

Whatever the conductor says about the beat should be noted in the music. Sometimes just writing "in 2" or "in 8" is enough. But I have found stroke marks (//) over each beat to be more versatile—and a clearer indication of where the beat is. I call these marks *strokes* for a definite reason: people who call them *slashes* tend to use them wildly, slashing clarity from the page. Just compare these two versions of a line from the viola part for Elliott Carter's Variations for Orchestra:

This slashed version, above, implies that the movement is in four, but it doesn't tell anything else about where the beats are, or how the subdivisions fit in.

This second version (with a stroke over each beat) shows that the beat is four, shows where the beats are, and makes the subdivisions clearer.

In addition to the standard indications for fingering (Arabic numerals for fingers, Roman numerals for strings), I have found the following symbols to be very handy. They indicate changes of position and reaches of the fingers:

/ = shift upward
\ = shift downward
x = extend for this note
c = contract for this note

We all know how important the right fingering can be in a difficult passage. Technical problems sometimes melt away like magic when a good fingering has been thought of. And although theoretically correct fingerings also have to be practiced, a guiding number here or there can often speed up learning.

One example that I am very fond of is a short scale from the viola part of John Adams' opera *The Death of Klinghoffer,* which has just 16 notes, ten of them with accidentals. It is an eyeful, and a handful.

In fact, the first time I ever saw it, it was worse. Someone had tried to be helpful by adding fingerings:

That's why I don't believe in putting in too many finger numbers or redundant accidentals; they add to the confusion by giving more to read and think about. Fortunately, I was able to find a pattern whose symmetry made this scale quite accessible, so the fingering becomes:

That was satisfying—a genuine magic fingering.

The following excerpt will show how useful the signs for shifting and extension/contraction can be. It is taken from the opening of the Debussy Sonata for Flute, Viola, and Harp. The extension in bar 4 and the contraction in bar 5 allow the line to be sustained without any audible shift:

(Please note: Since an X is also the symbol for double sharp, care must be taken to keep the extension mark small and close to the fingering number, to avoid confusion.)

The skull (crossbones optional) gives warning of a trap. It is more a psychological sign than a musical sign; it's meant to get your attention, and it does!

In general, the most precise way to avoid an accident is to put in a musical indication (clarify the beat, mark an extra accidental, write out the cue before your tricky entrance). But sometimes you simply need a wake-up call, and a skull does that just fine. I especially like to draw it over traps that other people have fallen into in rehearsals or previous performances. Others' mistakes can seed impressions in your subconscious that can come to life at the most embarrassing times. It's best to prevent that with a friendly smile.

The hold, or fermata, is usually printed like this: 𝄐 That's the way the fonts are sized; that's the way they get printed.

Pencils are more flexible than fonts. And since musical holds come in all lengths, the written holds can too:

Sometimes a conductor will say, "I might have to hold this; it depends on the stage action." In such cases of maybe–maybe not, I like to put in a "ghost" hold:

The fermata lends itself to ornamentations. Maybe that's because musicians have time on their hands while they are waiting for the hold to end. Here's a marking that has appeared in some parts when the whole orchestra is waiting for the tenor to finish his cadenza.

And since many European conductors refer to the fermata as a "corona," some of my colleagues have taken to drawing a mug of Mexican beer.

(This last is not a universally accepted convention.)

The first rule of orchestra playing is: Conductors like to be watched.

Almost any tempo or dynamic indication means, "Look at the conductor." But sometimes a special reminder is important. Maybe there's a spot where the conductor habitually stares at your section—for no reason, or for no apparent reason. It's usually a good idea to look back at a conductor who is staring at you.

The accepted reminder in these cases is a pair of spectacles.

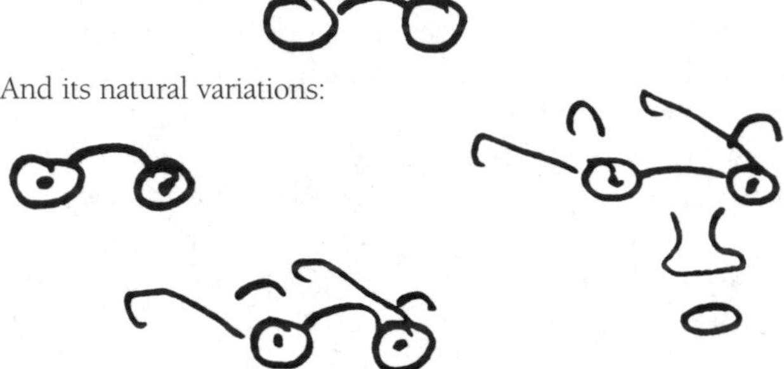

And its natural variations:

I recently found spectacles—with eye dots!—actually printed in some music. Here is that spot, from William Bolcom's *A Whiteman Tryptych*:

The comma, or caesura, can range in meaning (and size) from a brief phrase mark ' to a long full stop.

When it gets really big

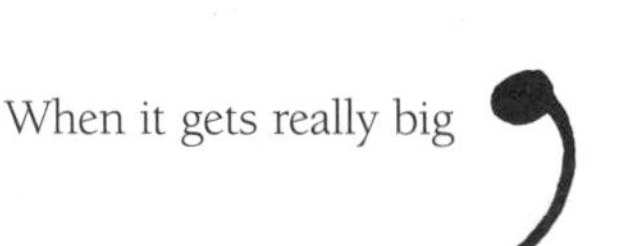

it can be replaced with so-called "Railroad Tracks": //

which can also signify a "Big Halt."

I prefer a big caesura to Railroad Tracks because one mark is easier to make than two, and because it is less likely to obscure the printed music beneath it.

‖: Reread this to confirm that the normal way repeats are printed is acceptable. :‖

Now reread this to confirm the value of adding wings.

It makes looking back easier to find and :‖ to read. ‖

These icons (= mute on, = mute off) show at a glance what has to be done with the mute, and where. Printed music usually indicates *con sordino, avec sourdine,* or *mit dampfer* right where it is time to play. Practical performers need more warnings. These symbols can be written in as soon as there is a chance to make the change: well before an entrance, for *con,* or right at the end of a passage, for *senza.*

The number-one reason for marking music, of course, is to make it easier to play. Bowings, dynamics, fingerings, warnings—they all help clarify the task at hand. They customize the road map. So far we have covered some of the practical markings an orchestral player can use, But humans can never be completely tied down to practicalities—we are too hungry for change, for variety. Wherever pencil and paper come together, more will happen than just "the task at hand." There will be invention.

Here is an example: When I joined the San Francisco Symphony in 1965, Josef Krips was the conductor, but the music and the music folders still carried residual signs of the nine-year directorship of Enrique Jordá, who had left just two years earlier. Many who had worked with Jordá praised his musical sensitivity, but they all admitted that he talked too much during rehearsals. (Often music would not be played in its entirety until the first performance!) His discourse was sprinkled with favorite phrases that my predecessors on Stand VI had turned into visual symbols on the music—among them were doorways, coffins, and wizards' hats:

This compelling introduction opened my mind to the values of personalized markings. They're more than fun. They're cultural transmission. They're historical record.

Here's another instance: In 1966 we performed *The Firebird* with Maestro Krips. In rehearsal, at the explosive chord that starts Kashchey's dance, Krips stopped the orchestra and shouted in his high-pitched voice, "I tell you somesink! Here it must sound as if a drop of fire were to fall on one!"

That seemed worth recording, so I wrote in the part: *Here it must sound as if a drop of fire were to fall on one.—J. Krips, December 1966.*

Krips' repertoire tended to repeat itself every two years. By 1968 I had advanced to Stand III, and we were doing *The Firebird* again. At the explosive chord that starts Kashchey's dance, Krips stopped the orchestra and shouted, "I tell you somesink! Here it must sound as if a drop of fire were to fall on one!"

I turned and waved to the sixth stand. They pointed to what they had just read and waved back. We had communicated.

Quoting conductors in the music has to be done very carefully, however. You can later miss notes while trying to understand what you're reading. An entry in the margin of a part to *Il trovatore* reads: *It is "I do not have the possibility from so much terror to speak."—D. Oren, 9/2/94.* This takes almost as long to figure out as the passage takes to play. But once you get used to it, the sense of hushed terror does indeed come through.

Any writing in the part should leave the musical text unmarred and easy to read. One enterprising San Francisco Opera Orchestra violist undertook to write an explanation of the complicated story of *La forza del destino* in her part. She kept the music clear, but the story went everywhere: around the margins, between the lines, and under the rests.

It was all too much for the person responsible for the music, and it led to the following written exchange on page 45:

Alvaro is wounded. He's going to die!

So is the cretin who scrawled the libretto all over this part!—Signed, the Librarian from Hell.

(The part still has the story written on it, though.)

String players are usually kept too busy in rehearsal for such extended projects. Our colleagues in the winds, brass, or percussion are more likely to have long rests to count, and they often have to "just sit there" while the conductor rehearses the violins. That's probably why the most elaborate sketches and drawings I've encountered come from nonstring players. They have more time.

Some use that time very well—even therapeutically. Anyone who has ever experienced recording anxiety will appreciate English hornist Raymond Duste's view of a San Francisco Symphony recording session of the "New World" Symphony, with its big English horn solo.

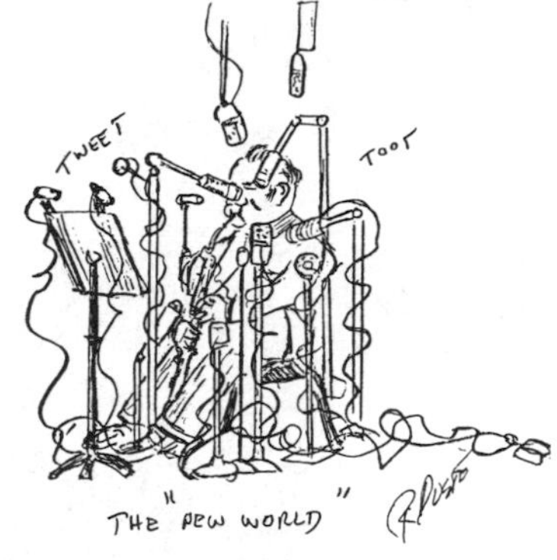

Emotionally expressive cartoons are not always so refined. The catalogue of destruction below implies boredom and anger. (I have been told that the lone victim of these attacks was meant to be the conductor of the evening.)

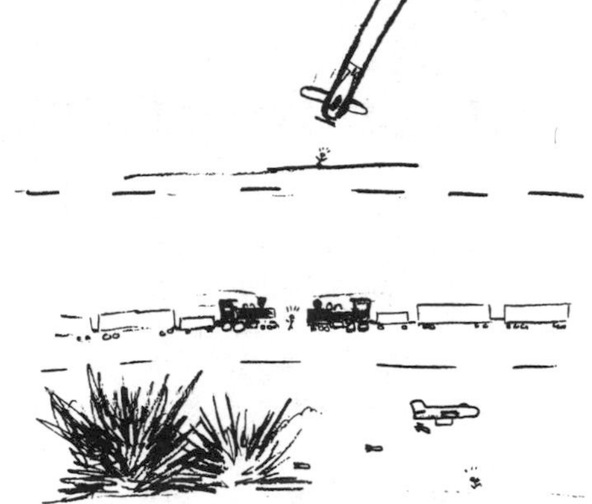

Not all drawings are so violent, but some do give warning of danger ahead. I think this elegant train on page 7 of the Horn III part to *Il trovatore* is meant to imply a possible "train wreck" in the music on that page.

Notice that the music to be played is still kept reasonably clear. (And look at all those rests! A rare sight for those of us in the string section.)

The following entry, also in *Il trovatore,* has a lot of dark psychological portent, but everyone who sees it smiles.

Since so many of the examples cited have come from San Francisco Opera music, it seems only right to end with clarinetist Greg Dufford's tribute to that company's late, great administrator, Kurt Herbert Adler.

All this is just an indication of how many ways there are to invent, express, and goof off during a rehearsal—as if it didn't come naturally. Seek your own way. You too can contribute to history.

(Special thanks to musician-cartoonists Raymond Duste, Brian McCarty, and Greg Dufford.)

In Praise of Prompters 24

THE AUDIENCE ALMOST NEVER SEES THEM, but the grateful singers always know they are there. At any performance, the man or woman who clambers into the prompter's box for the night takes on a great responsibility. The prompter is a force in the energy chain that keeps opera happening.

The prompter's box—that low, oblong turret in the center of the proscenium—is equipped for the work. Two closed-circuit TVs, one on the left and one on the right, show the conductor at the podium. There is a rack to hold the piano score of the opera, and a motorized seat that can be adjusted for height. The prompter looks and speaks out on the stage at foot level, through a window a little more than a foot high and three feet wide.

And from that humble location, the prompter helps manage and direct what takes place on the stage. Opera is rich and complicated, and the excitement and dangers of its live performances require a multilevel team effort. Even in its busiest and most crowded stage scenes, the actions of opera are subject to the rhythms and pace of the music. There is very little leeway. As the basso Paul Plishka once put it, "Just one instant of hesitation, and that orchestra is halfway down the block."

The prompter's work is to avert those hesitations by giving word cues and signals to indicate every vocal entrance just before it occurs—from the moment the singing starts until the end of the performance. It is demanding and difficult work that can often save the moment.

Jonathan Khuner is an experienced and thoughtful conductor and vocal coach who has many observations about the relationship between the prompter and the singers. His comments are based on a wide and varied practice as a staff member of the San Francisco Opera and music director of Berkeley Opera, and on his time as prompter at the Met and at Bayreuth.

"Throughout an opera, the prompter is the singer's best friend," Jonathan says, "someone who is there to help, encourage, and support. As with every relationship, this friendship is a two-way street, of course. Some people make friends more easily than others. Some work with the prompter and develop a good rhythm and pace. Others hold back—but the prompter is still there for them. Just by being in the box, we can sometimes give extra confidence and security to a young singer, or to a stand-in performing without rehearsal.

"The public thinks that we wait until something goes wrong and then try to help, but that would be far too late. We give every cue in advance, and not just for reasons of memory. The fact is, singers often cannot hear the orchestra. That seems strange: We hear it, why can't they? Well, when they stand midstage, 15 yards or more away from the pit, and let out those tremendous sounds that they can make, sometimes all they can hear is themselves. I've worked with Paul Plishka, for example. He's a great pro, and he knows exactly what he needs. He says, 'I need this word here, because when I come on stage I don't know where the hell the conductor is. And later I really need this entry, because the chorus has started to mill around me and it's hard to see anything.'

"Basically, the prompter is like the third-base coach in baseball. There are certain specific things on the field that he has to be aware of. The runner charging the base might also be aware of them, but he might not—and he wants a clear signal about whether to tag up or to accelerate toward home."

Jonathan adds, "It's the prompter's job to take care of this sort of thing, not the conductor's—he has lots of other things on his mind."

How the prompter handles that job can be very individual. Jonathan Khuner's quietly good-humored intelligence is valued wherever he works, but the job can lend itself to more flamboyant treatment.

Like that of Philip Eisenberg, for example. The 1988 recipient of San Francisco's prestigious Opera Medal made an impression that is still remembered. Quiet in personal conversation (though relentlessly persistent), in the prompter's box he could take off all the wraps.

When complex crowd scenes threatened to come unglued, Phil would bend them to his will. He would pound out the basic beat on the side of the box, shout word cues, thrust his hands out of the window, snap his fingers for attention, and energetically conduct the proceedings. He could be the most visible of prompters. It was a more expansive interpretation of the job than most, but it worked. It helped that he was right.

Conductor Sara Jobin intentionally chose to be low-key back when she was prompting. Quiet or not, her style once helped a singer get through a harrowing and heroic experience that vividly embodied some of the dangers (and a lot of the courage) of live performance.

"It was in 1999," says Sara, "and Ruth Ann Swenson was going to sing *Lucia di Lammermoor.* We rehearsed for several weeks. Ruth Ann and I developed a good working relationship, but then she got sick and had to cancel 24 hours before the opening night. They were able to get Tracy Dahl to come and sing the role, but she literally arrived the day before the performance. Her only rehearsal was the afternoon of the show. She first met the conductor at 7 PM and she was onstage at 8 PM.

"Now, Tracy had just had a baby a few months before. She hadn't sung any roles as big as *Lucia* during those months, and she hadn't done *Lucia* itself for a few years. She really watched me. You wouldn't have known it from the audience, but she had a way of flashing me a big white eyeball that showed she needed a cue.

"It worked. She got all the words, no tra-la-las. At the end of the show, when she was taking her bow, she almost dove toward me in the box and shook both my hands. My friends in the balcony were all excited: 'We saw your hands!' Afterward I saw her backstage, and she was really appreciative and grateful."

And Sara adds, "That's when I told her I had never prompted before."

25 Remembering Emile Férir

EMILE FÉRIR (1874–1947) was an eminent principal violist during the late 19th and early 20th centuries. His career was remarkable for both its distinction and its longevity. And yet, until recently, he had almost disappeared from the historical record, and from the memory of other violists.

I have received more information about Emile Férir through the generosity of Ruth Rumpler, the widow of Harry Rumpler. Harry—my friend, colleague, and former teacher—studied with Férir in Los Angeles during the 1930s. He inherited several items of Férir memorabilia that Ruth Rumpler has now passed on to me.

The material is a small treasure trove: an assemblage of photos, an autograph book, and a chronological outline of Férir's career, most likely compiled by his half-sister, Clemence Dieudonne. Fittingly, there is also a small treasure chest for the trove; some of the items came in an old wooden cigar box with a stenciled scene of "Giant Redwoods of California" on its top. The box belonged to M. Férir—a symbolic recognition of his California years.

This material helps us to get a clearer view of Férir's remarkable professional life. What follows is an overview based on Mlle. Dieudonne's summary, the short Férir biography in Volume I of Maurice Riley's *The History of the Viola,* and my own memories of stories that Harry Rumpler told me when I was studying with him in the early 1960s.

Emile Férir was born in 1874 (Riley states 1873, but I am inclined to take the word of Mlle. Dieudonne) near Brussels. He studied at the Brussels Conservatory—violin with Eugène Ysaÿe and viola with Léon Firket—in about 1888 and then continued his studies at the Paris Conservatory, graduating with a Medaille d'or in 1891.

Professional training was intense in those times, and the absence of radio or television opened plenty of time for practice. The Belgian violinist Ovide Musin records in his book, *My Memories* (Musin Publishing Co.), that in order to graduate with a gold or silver medal from the Conservatory at Liège in the 1870s, a candidate had to have ready a memorized repertoire of 15 pieces, from which the jury would select what it wanted to hear. Presumably, after such preparation, the successful candidate was ready to go to work.

It is certainly clear that Férir got started young, and that he traveled. He was principal violist of the Lamoureux Orchestra of Paris from 1892 to 1894 (starting at the age of 18), principal of the Scottish Symphony from 1894 to 1896 (George Henschel was conductor), and principal of the Queen's Hall Orchestra, under Henry Wood's direction, from 1896 to 1902.

Harry Rumpler once told me that Férir had been the viola soloist for the world premiere of Strauss' *Don Quixote,* and Maurice Riley, when I asked him to confirm, said that it seemed possible. The world premiere of that work was in Cologne in 1898, during Férir's years in the Queen's Hall Orchestra. It is reasonable to think that a distinguished virtuoso principal might have been invited to premiere a major soloistic work.

Harry Rumpler also told me another story that dates from those Queen's Hall years. Not all of the details are clear, but the gist of the story holds true to the known facts: In London, Férir acquired a bow by James Tubbs. Dated 1896, it was elegantly simple, with a plain ebony frog and gold mountings. Beautiful to look at, it also played beautifully. It was much admired by another member of the orchestra with a promising future: Lionel Tertis.

Tertis repeatedly offered to buy the bow; Férir repeatedly refused. And that remained the situation until there came a night when Férir needed some drinking money.

The low amount they agreed on was probably just part of the joke. Férir "sold" the bow to Lionel Tertis for one pound—and went out for the evening.

At the next payday, Férir had money again. But when he tried to "buy" back his bow, Tertis refused. And Tertis continued to refuse for some time—as though they were in a schoolyard game of keep-away. (Remember, Férir was just 22 when he got the bow, and Tertis was only 20. A few years later they were still young men. Boys will goof off, even boys who are going to be famous.) This situation continued until Férir received an invitation from Karl Muck to go to America and be principal violist of the Boston Symphony.

Now the tension reached a crisis: Férir was leaving England and the teasing had to end. Tertis understood that, and he agreed to sell the bow back . . . for *two* pounds.

I own that bow now. It passed from Férir to Harry Rumpler, and from Harry to me. It is magnificent, full of tone and spring. It improves the sound of every viola it plays. One pound? . . . Two pounds? . . . It was worth every penny!

Tertis does not mention any of this in his book *My Viola and I*, nor does he mention Férir. But he does describe how he had been "working at the viola" in his spare time while playing in the Queen's Hall orchestra as a second violinist, and that he was advanced to the position of principal violist in 1902, which is the year Férir was invited to America. All the facts fit.

Férir was principal of the Boston Symphony for 15 years, from 1903 to 1918. Riley mentions that Férir "frequently" performed the Cecil Forsythe Concerto, and other solo opportunities must also have come along. His solo playing seems to have made a powerful impression: Philip Hale, the critic of the *Boston Transcript,* referred to him in one review as "the outstanding string player of the Boston Symphony." High praise, indeed. (We have no way of knowing how the other fine string players of the Boston Symphony felt about that public comparison, but it wasn't Férir's fault that the critic seemed compelled to put his praise in competitive terms.)

The period from 1918 to 1921 was filled with a variety of musical experiences for Férir. He was principal in Stokowski's Philadelphia orchestra for one year. He toured Europe with Walter Damrosch and the New York Philharmonic in the summer of 1920. And he worked with Elizabeth Sprague Coolidge.

The history of chamber music in America—and the world—owes enormous gratitude to the generosity of Elizabeth Sprague Coolidge. (Walter Cobbett's *Cyclopedic Survey of Chamber Music* calls her "the Lady Bountiful of chamber music.") The late teens and early twenties of the 20th century saw the origins of her projects, with the beginning of the Berkshire Festival and the earliest of her composition contests.

According to Mlle. Dieudonne's chronology, Férir formed and played in the Coolidge Quartet under Mrs. Coolidge's patronage from 1919 to 1921. He often played in quartets made up of principal players of the various orchestras in which he played; Riley's short biography includes mention of the Kruse Quartet in London, the Arbos and Schroeder Quartets in Boston, and the Rich Quartet in Philadelphia.

And then, in 1921, he moved with his family to Los Angeles, to take over the principal post of the Los Angeles Philharmonic, which he held until his retirement in 1940. He died in San Clemente, California, in 1947.

During the Los Angeles years he also taught (Sven Reher and Harry Rumpler were two among his many students). He is remembered for his kindness and dedication in guiding his students' careers, as well as their educations. (Harry Rumpler also told me that the highest praise he bestowed was a quiet *"pas mal,"* or "not bad.")

Los Angeles was a musically busy city, famous for motion pictures and fine weather. It was a good place to maintain an orchestra career while attending to the family challenges of raising a learning-disabled son. But it was far away from the intense activities and print-media scrutiny of the East Coast. The move west might be a partial cause of Férir's being less well-remembered in viola history than he deserves to be.

I hope that this brief survey will help change that. Simply on the basis of his orchestral career, he deserves our memory and recognition. Further research will reveal more details, of course; but for now let us simply recall and respect the achievements and contributions of this dedicated violist. He was one of us, and a part of our history.

26 Felix Said

IN 1996, THE REGIONAL ORAL HISTORY OFFICE of the Bancroft Library at the University of California, Berkeley, published Felix Khuner's memoir, *A Violinist's Journey from Vienna's Kolisch Quartet to the San Francisco Symphony and Opera Orchestras.*

The book is about Felix Khuner, and what Felix said. Gathered and selected from interviews with him, it contains many of his words and much of his wisdom and his wit. It gives a glimpse of him the way a printed score gives a glimpse of the music. Those of us who worked with him, who took coachings from him, who respected, liked, enjoyed, and loved him, have memories that surround his words. We remember the vividness of his presence, the music of who he was.

But words definitely went along with that music. Felix is often quoted in the musical world he inhabited. In the San Francisco Bay Area, downstairs near the orchestra pit in War Memorial Opera House, backstage at Davies Symphony Hall, in carpools of musicians on their way to work, in string-teaching studios or in living rooms set up for playing chamber music, whenever a story begins with "Felix said..." musicians know who is meant.

And if someone doesn't know, we tell him. Felix Khuner is too important to us to be forgotten. We welcome the chance to share memories of this unique and distinctive man who influenced us so much—as performer, teacher, colleague, colorful character, and good friend.

During more than 50 years in the Bay Area, Felix said . . . a lot! His active, powerful mind was filled with memories, thoughts, and opinions that he expressed generously and energetically (sometimes, indeed, aggressively). His evaluations of music were based on deep knowledge. His appraisals of the musical world came out of long experience. His reminiscences of Europe, and of Viennese music and musicians from the period between the two World Wars—a period that seemed to some of us like legends from a distant, golden time—were for him a part of living, personal memory.

We listened to those memories with interest and gratitude. And they took on an extra aura for us, because of what we knew about his amazing musical memory.

It was famous. Fabulous! Even people who didn't know him had heard of it. His years with the Kolisch String Quartet, playing the canon of Western quartet music by memory, gave his reputation an authority that pushed our respect toward awe.

Or toward incredulity. Musicians new to the Bay Area found his reputation hard to believe. They looked for evidence. Felix had retired from the San Francisco Symphony by 1972, but he was still being engaged as an extra player and substitute. At the start of the year, young Barbara Riccardi, then a new member of the orchestra, found herself sitting at the back of the second violin section next to an elderly man who clearly knew what he was doing.

The program that week was especially challenging, and at one rehearsal some of the other young musicians who had recently joined the orchestra gathered around Barbara during an intermission to ask, "OK, you can settle this once and for all. Does he really know the second violin part of *Verklärte Nacht* by heart?"

"Yes, he really does," Barbara answered, "And what's more, he expects me to know it, too. He never turns pages!"

Later that same week, as the Schoenberg was being rehearsed, some questions about individual notes and the accuracy of the printed music began to come up. Then the depth of Felix's knowledge was made even clearer. When Maestro Seiji Ozawa himself wasn't sure how to answer some of the inquiries, voices from the orchestra started saying, "Ask Felix, Felix knows." And Felix answered the questions from his substitute seat at the back of the second violin section, commenting on how the harmonies were different in similar passages, correcting notes when necessary, playing violin lines, woodwind lines, bass lines on his violin. Felix knew, with a depth and passion that is more than memory. He knew the music by heart—the hold of a lifelong love.

(By the end of that rehearsal, the conductor seemed afraid to do anything interpretative without asking Felix's permission.)

If Felix's abilities sound like those of a musical superhero, his daily self-presentation was more like a musical Clark Kent. He was five feet, five inches tall, with a halo of white hair—thick on the sides, thin on top—and glasses. His clothing was a statement of very personal tastes in style . . . and economics. The yellow windbreaker he liked so much lasted for close to 20 years. His high-water pant cuffs often showed an expanse of white socks above scuffed brown shoes. (He sometimes wore those shoes into the Opera House pit for performances, a comfortable adjunct to his white-tie-and-tails formal wear—tails that he often carried rolled up in a brown paper shopping bag.) His silver-colored metal lunch box seemed to have an unlimited supply of cold, dry toast—his most frequent snack. And his violin case, of the classic "Are-you-carrying-a-machine-gun-in-there?" shape, had been repaired so often with black tape that there were many who questioned whether any of the original material remained.

Though his appearance was unprepossessing, only a few minutes with him revealed the scope and energy of his intellectual interests. He was rereading Schiller, he was studying Japanese, he was (again) climbing Koltanowski's problem-solving ladder in the *San Francisco Chronicle* chess column, he was listening to the Giants baseball game on a small transistor radio held next to his ear, he had just written an angry letter to a local newspaper to express his views and feelings on a matter of politics.

He expressed his views and feelings on all matters that were important to him. Whether talking about musical values or political opinions or a recent trade by the Giants, Felix said what he had to say with a vigor that could approach aggressiveness. (He might take a position opposed to yours just to test the firmness of your conviction.) Those of us who remember his voice and movements know how animated he could become. As his gestures became larger and more intense, his gentle Viennese accent moved from calm to excited, from musical to shrill.

What Felix said was important—and how he said it was a vital part of the meaning. It would be unfair to his complexity not to mention that some people found his range of intensities abrasive; some students found him hard to take.

Felix was much more than an abstract intellect. He was a rich and complex human being—wise, contentious, musical, thoughtful, impetuous, annoying, kindly. Even those who were not completely comfortable with him acknowledged that Felix was colorful.

And for those of us who were comfortable with him, Felix was fun!

He knew it, too, and could joke about himself. On a Saturday at midnight in 1970, when he was still a member of the San Francisco Symphony, the orchestra's charter bus returned a group of tired musicians to the Opera House after a concert in Cupertino. Felix was the first out of his seat near the back of the bus. Hugging his violin case, his metal lunch box, and the brown paper shopping bag with his rolled-up tailcoat, Felix pressed purposefully down the aisle, saying, "Excuse me, excuse me, please. I have to get off first. I have students waiting for lessons at my home, and afterwards we are playing chamber music."

We laughed, because we knew it wasn't true; and we laughed because we knew it could have been. Some major themes of his life—chamber music, teaching, home, and a sense of restless hurry—were all present in his joke. (It's surprising that he didn't mention gardening.) He had a tremendous capacity for work, and a way of filling the niches of his busy schedule with students.

Which leads to other stories: Felix said that he had planned to sleep late one Sunday morning but was awakened by the doorbell at 9 AM. He answered, and there was one of his adult students, quite surprised to find his tousle-haired teacher in pajamas and bathrobe. "Did I get the schedule wrong?" he asked. "I thought we had an appointment for a violin lesson this morning."

"We do," Felix said. "If you brought money, I am prepared to teach."

Felix also said, "I told one of my students that she had made a mistake and that I would play the passage the way she had played it; she should listen for the mistake and tell me what it was. When I played it, she said, 'You were out of tune.'

"Yes, that's right, but that's not what I meant. Here, I'll play it again."

"Your bow bounced on the string crossing."

"Yes, yes, okay! But that's not it! Here, I'll do it once more."

"You scratched."

"ALL RIGHT! ALL RIGHT! ALL THAT IS TRUE, BUT WHAT I WANTED YOU TO NOTICE WAS THE MISTAKE IN RHYTHM!"

"What mistake in rhythm?"

With colleagues, as well as with students, associating with Felix had a learning component. Playing chamber music with him was a great experience. He saw past printed notes to the meaning of the music, the individuality of each piece, and he led with a freedom and breadth of phrasing that was enlightening.

Those sessions could also have surprising moments. His sense of impatience really showed when he said, "This is the 20th century! We have all heard these motifs before. We will play the Minuet without repeats."

Each memory of what Felix said, and of who he was, leads to other memories. The things that Felix said keep their freshness. They stay in memory, verbal talismans and teaching stories that keep on doing their work.

Like what Felix said about teaching: "The teacher's work is to watch the student, and listen to the student, and then use what he has seen and heard to sense in his own body how it must feel to play and sound like the student. And then to compare that feeling with how he normally feels when he himself plays. And then to use every means in his power to convey that difference to the student."

Like what Felix said when a colleague once asked, "What is this 'musical value' that you keep talking about? We need to play the notes. We need to put on a good show. What else are you talking about?"

And Felix said, "Don't worry about it. If you aren't driven to find it, just let it go. You can live a perfectly decent life without concerning yourself about it—millions do.

"But if you really want to know what it is, if you really must find it and experience it, then you will seek it everywhere you can. You will not be able to stop. You will look for it and listen for it, and think about it. You will make up your mind about it, and then change your mind—and then change it again! But you will always seek it."

A musician's credo.

The last time I saw Felix, at the corner of University and Shattuck Avenue in Berkeley, he expressed himself with all the verve and acerbity that he ever had. Our encounter was accidental, and I was glad to see him: "Hi, Felix!"

"Ah, Heimberg. Have you heard the condition of my health?"

"Why no, I. . . ."

"Lung cancer." He nodded. "Possible metastasis to the brain." He wrinkled his nose and tapped his temple with his index finger. "I am angry with my HMO. If they had not stopped the multiphasic examination a few years ago we might have caught it earlier . . . but then again, maybe not." He shrugged. "Eighty-four isn't bad, huh?"

I couldn't answer. My voice was choked, my eyes were misted with tears. "Felix, I—"

"Listen, I have to go. I have some things to do. Good seeing you." And he left.

Two weeks later he left us all, with our cherished memories of who he was: the man, his music, and—of course—what he said.

Considering Kreisler

27

THERE IS A BIOGRAPHY OF NOTE for the Kreisler fan on your list. Amy Biancolli's 1998 *Fritz Kreisler: Love's Sorrow, Love's Joy* (Amadeus Press) is a beautiful book, well-researched, carefully thought-out, and compellingly written. It is a fine tribute and memorial to the great violinist whose musicianship and charm so entranced music lovers from the late 19th century through the first half of the 20th.

In her preface, Biancolli gives two reasons for writing the book. "My first is the simplest and, I believe, the most persuasive," she tells us. "I wrote a new biography of Fritz Kreisler because I fear he is in danger of being forgotten." Forgotten? At first reading it seems unlikely, but Biancolli has a precise meaning in mind when she writes this.

It is certainly true that Kreisler's name is still known, and that his compositions are played by every violin student. But many of his distinctive musical and personal qualities may no longer be in the public's awareness. He was a man of feeling and philosophy who believed that "art ought to be a priesthood, and every artist should be a priest."

That is how he felt and how he conveyed music, and that is what might be forgotten. Contemporary audiences (and many contemporary violinists) may not be attuned to, in Biancolli's words, "his deeply human playing, and his mystical relation with the instrument."

Kreisler's beautiful music making defined an aesthetic for the 20th century. The desire to reemphasize his musical qualities in our collective memory would have been reason enough for writing this book, but Biancolli had another motive as well: the quest for historical truth. While paying great respect to Louis Lochner's 1950 authorized biography, *Fritz Kreisler* (second edition by Paganiniana Publications, 1981), she points out that it was written under the tight constraint of Harriet Kreisler's editorial review and censorship.

Biancolli's paragraph on this subject deserves to be quoted in full, because it delineates some of the differences between this book and Lochner's earlier work.

> This brings me to my second reason [for writing this book]: Lochner's biography, as exhaustive as it is, contains some glaring

> (and fascinating) gaps. Because Kreisler's wife, Harriet, served as censor for the final manuscript, the volume fails to describe with any candor either Harriet's control over her husband's life or the intense dislike she aroused in nearly everyone she met. It also overlooks the matter of Kreisler's ethnic and religious heritage and the complex forces behind his flight from Germany in the late 1930s. On the flip side, Lochner's biography at times contains too much—Kreisler was an infamous fibber, and several of the yarns spun in those pages are prevarications of the most thoroughly spurious sort. Many of them are by their very natures impossible to confirm or debunk, but I have done my best (in a chapter dedicated to the subject and throughout the rest of the book) to examine them with a critical eye and a good-natured appreciation of their literary worth.

Good-natured appreciation is an important trait of this work. Biancolli admires Kreisler just as much as Lochner did. Of course, he was an admirable man. He was broadly cultured, as a student of the classics (when he awoke from a monthlong coma after being hit by a truck in 1941, he could at first speak only Latin and ancient Greek), a two-year medical student who loved gathering early medical texts into his rare-book collection, a linguist, a composer, and an international ambassador of musical goodwill.

He was also "at core an easygoing, unambitious man who, were it not for a practical and highly ambitious wife, would have spent his days with friends and his money on long shots. He enjoyed drinking, eating, gambling, socializing, and a good tale, engagingly told."

And here is the contribution Biancolli makes: She draws connections between Kreisler's noble public image as a musical high priest and the very endearing—and fallible—human being he actually was.

Making those connections is a complex task. To accomplish it, the author devised an appropriate structure for her work, claiming from the start that it is about the artist's legacy as much as about his accomplishments. "The structure of the book reflects this emphasis on context," she writes. "Unlike Lochner's biography, which provided a straight chronology of Kreisler's career, mine is more analytical and less linear. Although the chapters are organized in a loosely chronological manner, many sections are topical in nature and function as essays rather than direct accounts of Kreisler's life."

The text is divided into 14 chapters, each dealing with a specific theme (and eschewing clever chapter headings in favor of titles that actually let you know what the theme is). Some examples: "Vienna" (a searching and rhapsodic description of Kreisler's native city), "Fritzi and

Harriet" (a not-at-all rhapsodic description of the Kreislers' domestic relations), and "Kreisler and Heifetz" (an examination of the famous pair, summed up marvelously with the observation that "perhaps Oscar Shumsky was correct—perhaps Heifetz was the century's greatest violinist and perhaps Kreisler was its greatest musician").

Since the book progresses in a sequence that is not a bowstroke-by-bowstroke recounting of Kreisler's life, it offers byways for thought and contemplation, a reflective meandering. Sometimes certain descriptions or opinions occur in more than one chapter, but that is a natural effect of dealing with themes that are laced throughout the subject's life.

I will not summarize this book any further. It is rich and thought-provoking, and the reader can enjoy its complexity. But I do want to offer a few personal comments on some of its observations.

In Chapter Six ("Tall-Tale Teller: The Kreisler Apocrypha"), Biancolli addresses the violinist's "love of mythic hyperbole" and "the breezy manner in which Kreisler manufactured historical source references for what were probably his own conceits." One of the anecdotes she discusses is Kreisler's claim that he influenced the composition of Arnold Schoenberg's *Verklärte Nacht* by advising the young composer to change it from a heavily double-stopped trio to a sextet.

I've played that sextet, and the unlikelihood of the story is built into its difficult score. In fact, the notion is pretty funny. Biancolli hedges her evaluation of the story's truth: "This claim of Kreisler's might be true. It might also be false, the probability of which increases when one understands that the story is not only impossible to confirm but is just the sort of yarn that Kreisler loved to tell."

I did a little informal research of my own on this subject, asking Jonathan Khuner, the son of Felix Khuner of the Kolisch String Quartet, if he had ever heard the story. Jonathan's direct connection to that period of Viennese musical history carries some weight, and he had never heard it—not from his father, not in his studies. It gave him a good laugh.

"Fritzi and Harriet" is a fascinating and perplexing chapter—a chapter that lasted all of Kreisler's adult life (the pair were married for 60 years, counting from the first of their four wedding ceremonies). Human beings have always been curious about one another's private lives, and Kreisler's relationship with his wife was puzzling—and often annoying—to many of his contemporaries. Biancolli addresses the subject with dignity, compassion, and truthfulness.

The anecdotes related here do not make Harriet Kreisler more likable. Her nursing and charitable activities in World War I were honorable, certainly, but on a social and personal level, she could be very hard to take. Even as a young boy, I heard stories from musically connected adults about Harriet Kreisler's brash and domineering style. This book also contains stories of her public rudeness and explosive anger, her embarrassing insults to her husband and his work. The stories describe a very self-indulgent, bad-mannered woman.

But they imply more. They suggest psychological dynamics that are almost diagnosable: The alternations of volatility and debilitating illness, which sent her to a sickbed for months at a time, sound from this distance like an untreated manic-depressive syndrome. The closest Biancolli (or anyone I've ever read) comes to suggesting this is in her reference to Harriet's "frequent, and usually vague, illnesses . . . from severe bouts of influenza to a condition that sounds possibly psychosomatic."

Biancolli does offer a psychological slant on the endurance of this marriage of complete opposites. "From one perspective, Kreisler's attachment to his domineering spouse made perfect sense, for it echoed [his father] Salomon Kreisler's decades-long marriage to the short-tempered Anna. . . . Anna and Harriet were both practical women, both prone to rages, both ill (Anna chronically; Harriet often), both unmusical, both capable of violence, and both wholly, undeniably devoted to their husbands. It sounds hackneyed and almost quaintly Freudian to say so, but Fritz Kreisler married his mother." The suggestion is made carefully, but it is compelling.

Was Harriet Kreisler hard to live with? Obviously. But Kreisler loved her. And he valued her place in his life. "Everything I am as a violinist I owe to Harriet," he said, as quoted in the book. Biancolli comments on this: "It is entirely possible, although some more ardent Kreisler devotees may deny it, that without Harriet Kreisler there to nudge him—to needle him into practicing, to raise his fees, to protect him from the masses—Fritz Kreisler would not have had his career." And she goes on to point out that, despite his great talents, "he was not nearly as ambitious as Harriet and seemed to prefer the company of friends, the dusty comfort of antique books, and the thrills of the poker table to anything approaching hard work."

We could speculate about these mysteries for a lifetime, and this book is an excellent starting place.

Music for Viola and Piano (and Bird and Child) 28

ONE MIDWEEK EVENING in the midst of a busy opera season, my friend Jonathan Khuner and I enjoyed a special treat. We spent several hours together reading recent music for viola and piano.

As members of the San Francisco Opera (he on its musical staff, I in the viola section), we kept professionally busy with opera. But somehow each of us managed to free up a night for "the other" kind of music.

I have to qualify that. The evening was not completely free. Jonathan's wife Jillian, a fine singer, was away at a rehearsal, so we two men were in charge of lovely, lively Cecily Khuner, soon to be four years old, and her newly acquired cockatiel, Jake. You get the picture: two grown men taking care of one highly intelligent four-year-old. The balance of authority was almost even; the balance of available energy was definitely in Cecily's favor.

Because of her own commitments to the world of opera, Cecily was to be awake with us all evening. She was scheduled to perform in *Madama Butterfly* as the child "Trouble'" (an important nonsinging role), and she needed practice in staying up late.

So our preparation was shaped by the circumstances: We talked with Cecily, gathered together some picture books and toys where she could get to them easily, and fixed herbal tea for everyone except Jake, who got a handful of broken crackers. Then we left our charges in the kitchen and went to the living room, where we spread our stack of music on the floor—the traditional sorting place for stacks of music—and performed a reading triage.

We planned to start with material that was comfortably within reach and then go on to more difficult works, keeping at it as long as we could. We also agreed that we would look for opportunities to make positive comments about the music we were sampling. After all, it wouldn't be the composer's fault if we didn't "get it" right away, or if we were unable to read a work at first sight. We put our teacups on the hi-fi speakers and began.

It's always best to warm up on something simple, and this evening we had a perfect choice at hand. Lee Hoiby's *Ciaconetta* (Theodore Presser 114-40656) is dedicated "for Cecily Fortesque on her birthday." We called Cecily in from the kitchen to listen. This lovely little work, just 46 measures and three minutes long, is pleasant and melodious, and within the technical reach of intermediate players. It would serve well as a student work or could provide an encore or interlude in a program that needs a short, quiet moment. (Cecily thought that the "Cecily" part of the dedication was nice, that Fortesque was a strange name, and that the piece itself was pretty. Then she wanted to go back to the kitchen.)

Introduction et allegro, by Chantal Auber (Editions Durand SA D&F 14684), is considerably more demanding but still quite playable for intermediate players approaching the advanced level. Its straightforward melodiousness and the rhythmic variety of the Allegro are appealing; this first reading gave the impression that, with study, a dedicated interpreter would find a good deal of color and range in the work.

Jacques Charpentier's *Couleurs pour une sonate imaginaire* (Editions Musicales Alphonse Leduc AL.28.218) has harsh harmonies and lots of left-hand "scrambling" for the viola. It tests some of the technical resources of the player—as befits a piece written for a conservatory *concours*. It created a stark atmosphere from the very first chord—which spanned a wide range of the keyboard and then resolved to sustained harmonies, into which the viola entered, commenting with melodic fragments, double-stops, and arpeggiations. This work would add modern spice to a recital, but it would have to be placed carefully in the program. It is serious and strident, not sufficiently "listener-friendly" to be a starting piece.

Now, worried that things were just a little too quiet in the kitchen, Jonathan excused himself to check on Cecily and Jake. They were just fine. Jake, perched on the back of a chair, nibbled his cracker crumbs. Cecily was seated at the table looking at a book. What high talent! No wonder she is acting in *Madama Butterfly.*

For a change of pace, we then turned to two arrangements of well-known works transcribed for viola (or cello) and guitar: Dvořák's *Humoresque* and Saint-Saëns' *Le Cygne* (Editio Musica Budapest Z 13 970 and Z 13 969). Both are interesting settings of familiar pieces in an unfamiliar combination. Of the two, *Humoresque* seemed to work best. The guitar does not have the range of a piano, and the necessary compromises in chord voicings were more apparent in the Saint-Saëns.

At this point in the evening, Cecily—who had been very patient so far—decided it was time for us to play with her. For the next 20 minutes we three sat on the floor playing "Race to the Roof." (I will not review the game at this time, but I will mention that Cecily recognizes and counts numbers at a level that is a year ahead of what the child-development books predict. That comes in handy in a board game propelled by the roll of dice. Jonathan and I did okay at counting, too, and with a little more training we might get to be as adept at Cecily at crawling around on the floor.) When Cecily agreed to let us go back to playing music, some good discoveries were waiting for us.

Fantasy, by Frederick Koch (Southern Music Company SU 240), dedicated to violist Paul Neubauer, is a real keeper. The free and declamatory arpeggios and lyric melody are well woven together to create a work that has its own "mental space," truly a fantasy that is consistent and affecting. Periodically, the pianist reaches into the piano to dampen strings by hand, creating special sound-color effects and adding variety to the musical texture. As a short display piece, it would be very effective. And it sounds harder to play than it is! I always admire that in a display piece.

The biggest find of our evening was Thomas Pasatieri's *Sonata for Viola and Piano* (Subito Music Publishing, distributed by Theodore Presser, 494-02025), dedicated to Donald McInnes, who gave the work its first performance, with the composer at the piano. Jonathan was familiar with some of Pasatieri's operatic work, and he specifically wanted to hear this piece. I'm glad he did. It is an exciting work with lots of rhythmic drive, from the very beginning *Allegro molto* through the lyric *Andante cantabile* and *Lento* of the second movement to the *Allegro violento* of the third. We didn't reach full tempo at all times on this first reading. When we do, it will have even more energy and direction. I look forward to learning and performing it.

There was still plenty of music on the floor—and much of it looked interesting—but it would have to wait. By this time, it was 11 o'clock. Bright-eyed Cecily admitted that it might be time for bed. And Jonathan and I were definitely tired. (It must have been that game of "Race to the Roof.")

John Cage once wrote that it was not his purpose to erase the line between art and life, or even to blur the line between art and life: it was to show that there is no line between art and life. Evenings that combine child care and an exploration of music also make that point—strongly and beautifully. We all had a good time. Jonathan and I hope to try more music again soon, if it's OK with Cecily.

29 Letter from Backstage

THE GUARNERI STRING QUARTET played in the San Francisco Bay Area in October 1999, as it has for nearly three decades. Its annual fall visits here have always been important musical events. Whether playing in San Francisco's Herbst Theatre, Berkeley's Zellerbach Hall, or Stanford University's Dinkelspiel Auditorium, the Guarneri always fills the house with loyal—and satisfied—lovers of quartet music.

But this year was different. The advertisements announced that this was to be the group's last West Coast concert with David Soyer as cellist. The Guarneri String Quartet—which had performed with the same personnel since 1963—was going to change.

The change was not cataclysmic. It was planned as carefully as a musical change of tempo. There would be a period of transition as the distinguished cellist Peter Wiley, a longtime personal and musical friend of the quartet, became a member of the group. Soyer would continue to play in concerts on the East Coast, close to home, while Wiley took over during tours.

But that was to be the future, while the last West Coast performance with David Soyer was now. I wanted to be close to it in some way. I've known the Guarneri Quartet for many years; its returns to the Bay Area are opportunities to visit with friends as well as to hear their music. I knew that I would not be able to attend the concert that evening (I would be playing in the San Francisco Opera Orchestra for *Lucia di Lammermoor,* just across the courtyard in the Opera House), but I did want to hear at least some part of their work. So when I found out that they were having a touch-up rehearsal of one of their programmed pieces an hour and a half before the concert, I took advantage of the chance to sit in the empty hall and listen.

Herbst Theatre is a lovely place, decorated with murals and bright with gilt. When it's filled with an audience, it has a good performance sound; when it's empty, the added resonance makes it even better. The piece being rehearsed was Brahms' Quintet in G Major, Op. 111. The group was placed on the stage so that Soyer sat in the middle, looking out, looming over his cello like an intense, musical Vincent Price (for whom he has sometimes been mistaken). From where I sat, the proscenium lights created a strange effect as they reflected off the shiny floor of the stage and cast the players' shadows above them, upside down on the backdrop. Every action that a live musician made on stage was copied, at the speed of shadow, by an inverted musician floating in the air behind the group.

Ida Kavafian, who played second viola, has performed and recorded with the Guarneri before. Her sound fitted right in with the renowned lush tone that the quartet has always had. And she seemed quite at home with the outspoken rehearsal climate for which it is famous.

It's a climate that has frightened some and inspired others. Early in their combined career, the quartet members decided not to let outsiders attend their rehearsals. First violinist Arnold Steinhardt explains, "We had agreed to save time and get straight to work by delivering our musical comments without any efforts toward conventional politeness. But we didn't want strangers listening to us. They wouldn't understand. We didn't want to hear rumors: 'They hate each other! They're breaking up!' It was just never true."

More recently, they have relaxed their policy and even offered open rehearsals to the public. A few years ago, during the question period of one such event in San Francisco, a member of the audience said, "I am really impressed by the quality of communication that goes on among you. Is this the way you always are, or are you adding something for the audience?"

There was a brief moment of reflection, and then first violinist Arnold Steinhardt replied, "This is pretty much it. This is the way we are."

They are still that way. In the Herbst rehearsal, Steinhardt declared, "This is boring. The tempo is too slow."

"We can try it a little faster," replied Soyer, "but it should be heavy-footed, not light and running."

"Could you please play softer here?" asked Kavafian. "I can't hear myself."

"Can't hear yourself? Play louder!" Soyer said. "That's been the Guarneri motto for 30 years. We got it from Sascha Schneider at Marlboro."

Violist Michael Tree laughed and said conspiratorially to Kavafian, "Let's really give it to them the next time." Second violinist John Dalley smiled.

It was warmly satisfying to see and hear them at work again. I first knew about the Guarneri Quartet before it had a name; Steinhardt had been a friend of mine since junior high school. In the early 1960s, he told me about his summers of chamber music at Marlboro, and of how he and three other guys were thinking of forming a quartet. Schneider and the other members of the Budapest Quartet were very encouraging. There was a lot of work to do, but the prospects looked good. The future was exciting, promising, and uncertain, all at the same time.

Work and uncertainty preceded the group's successes, but it did have success—great success. Anyone who wants to fast-forward from those early times through 36 years of the quartet's history can find plenty of reference material: more than 50 CDs and recordings, reviews from all around the world, a motion picture (*High Fidelity*), and several books (including Steinhardt's beautiful memoir, *Indivisible by Four*). Those same four guys have continued their great commitment to chamber music and to each other. The process has worked wonderfully well for more than a third of a century.

But life—and music—are processes that happen in time, and time works its changes on us all. After several million miles of travel and concertizing, Soyer was tired of touring, even though he had "the constitution of an ox," in Steinhardt's words. It's not surprising. As Steinhardt says in *Indivisible by Four,* "It is exhausting work to practice, play a concert, travel with instruments and luggage, and then pick up your tired body, day after day, to repeat the process."

"Don't try to intellectualize away fatigue!" one of my teachers once admonished me during a lesson. Soyer backed up the advice once, when I congratulated him after an unusually long concert. He answered with the friendly directness that he is known for. "Thank you, Tom. It's a very difficult program, very demanding. Everything hurts. My hair hurts." He laughed. "Can you tell that to the audience? You play Mozart and your hair hurts?"

I don't think he has ever tried to tell that to an audience. But sometimes he's had occasion to speak about other things. At Zellerbach Hall just a few years ago, he stood at the edge of the stage and announced a change in the performance: The printed program was in error and the Mozart Quartet would not be played. Instead, the group would present one by Haydn. Suddenly his famous directness turned into his famous gruffness as he glared at the front rows. "Who hissed?" he demanded. "Haydn is a good composer!" And he turned back to his seat, shaking his head. The audience applauded.

At the Herbst rehearsal, I stayed as long as I could before going to my own performance, but the evening was not over when I left. Later, during the first intermission of *Lucia di Lammermoor,* a small group of musicians—friends, fans, former students—decided to run across the courtyard through the cool night air to try to catch some of the Guarneri performance from backstage.

It was a strange raid, a handful of people in formal dress tiptoeing through the backstage door—only to find that the quartet was also having an intermission! If there had been refreshments handy, there would have been strong temptation to turn the concert into a party. As it was, a party atmosphere was present, though with a time limit, since the program had to be completed. There were hugs and handshakes and quickly told anecdotes.

And there was silliness. I had brought a novelty, a metal mute attached to a flexible strip of metal topped with a small metal ball. When the strip wavers, it gives the instrument a strange, Theremin-like wail of a vibrato. Steinhardt tried it. "Arnold," said Soyer, "you've never sounded better."

The backstage managers were nervously looking at their watches. The audience was waiting. "We really should get started again." The talk quickly subsided (very professional!), the quintet went on stage, and the rest of us listened to the opening bars of the Brahms before leaving.

"Well," said Associate Principal Violist Sergei Rakitchenkov as we walked back to our opera, "it was symbolic listening." Symbolic listening to honor a great quartet. The best kind of honor for musicians.

By our second intermission, the other concert was over and its audience had dispersed. The last West Coast Guarneri String Quartet concert with David Soyer as cellist had taken place.

30 Puccini's Viola of Love

PUCCINI WROTE MUSIC FOR THE VIOLA D'AMORE only once in his career, as part of the poignant "Humming Chorus" in *Madama Butterfly.* This tender melody—just 48 measures long—represents the anguished night (*la notte angosciosa*) in which Cio-Cio-San waits for Pinkerton's return. During her vigil, Puccini treats the onstage tableau with inspired musical understatement: The orchestra in the pit quiets to a muted *ppp*, and backstage the unseen chorus vocalizes wordlessly, accompanied by a lone viola d'amore.

This solo accompaniment is not prominent, but it does add to the musical texture of the moment. Puccini, the great orchestrator—the man who put the bells of Castel Sant'Angelo onstage in *Tosca* and the sounds of bleating sheep in the woodwind section in *Suor Angelica*—created a delicate effect by using this ancient, beautiful instrument.

Though overshadowed by the more outspoken violin family for more than two centuries, the viola d'amore has a long, honorable history. It was widely popular in Europe in the 17th and 18th centuries, and Mozart's father, Leopold, commented in his *Treatise on the Fundamental Principles of Violin Playing* (1756), "It is a distinctive kind of fiddle which sounds especially charming in the stillness of the evening."

It is distinctive, to be sure, and it has a startling appearance. ("That's quite a piece of machinery you've got there," San Francisco Opera's Music Director Donald Runnicles said once about a d'amore I was holding.) It has at least 12 strings—three times as many as the more familiar violin or viola. The six that stretch over the bridge are played upon, and the six drone strings—thin and high-pitched—stretch under the bridge, to vibrate sympathetically with the chords and melodies being played.

Along with this ringing lyre of strings comes a pegbox bristling with tuning pegs. And instead of a curling scroll, every authentic d'amore carries a carved, blindfolded Cupid's head—an assertion of the theme of love. The mysterious murmur of those sympathetically vibrating strings gives the d'amore a special role in the "Humming Chorus." True, an instrument helps singers hold their intonation, a practical concern that any composer would consider—but a violin or viola or the familiar backstage harmonium could do that job equally well. The echoing ring of the d'amore adds an exotic overtone to the dramatic moment.

At Puccini's request, the great Italian luthier Leandro Bisiach built a viola d'amore in 1904 specifically for *Madama Butterfly*. That instrument is currently in the Museo degli Strumenti Musicali in Milan, Italy. Its label proudly declares that it was made expressly for *Madama Butterfly*, and Bisiach's heirs have a note from Puccini in which he states (in translation): "I have tried it in *Butterfly* and am extremely pleased." Another example, among many, of Puccini getting exactly what he wanted.

I have played this d'amore solo at the San Francisco Opera dozens of times. The adventure always begins by leaving the pit before the "Flower Duet." One advantage to sitting in the viola section near the pit exit is that there is less to stumble over on my way out. Nearby colleagues help by tilting bows and instruments away from me, horn players swivel on their chairs to make room, trumpet players pull back their music stands to clear a path. Backing down the wooden stairs to the narrow entryway we call the "Torpedo Room," I slip out the door and into the hallway.

A wall outside the pit is lined with shelves holding instrument cases. I wipe the rosin dust off my viola and tuck it in its case. Then I turn to the d'amore. Although I have played this solo many times, no performance can ever be routine. The viola d'amore not only looks different from a viola, it feels different, too. The strings are tuned in chords rather than in even intervals, the notes are farther apart along the string, and the fingerboard is wider, which affects both bowing and fingering. The solution to these challenges is, as always, practice. But even well-prepared, I always feel an edge of excitement on performance evenings. And the most exciting moment is when I open the d'amore's case: Will any strings be broken? How out of tune will it be?

Our wonderful harpist Olga Rakitchenkov once shared her philosophy about strings with me. In her mellifluous Russian accent, she said, "Take it from me, Tom, the more you have, the more they break." Sometimes a quick string change is needed, but d'amores *always* have to be tuned. Their strings are stressed by multiple tensions and bends; something always slips and has to be brought back to pitch.

After tuning, it's a quick trip through underground hallways and stairs that lead to the stage. Over the years, the chorus and I have been placed in many locations around the backstage area for the "Humming Chorus"—including a walkway three stories high. Recently we have been situated downstage right, near the stage manager's console (on the left of the stage, from the audience's point of view). Backstage there is a contrast between the electricians' 21st-century lighting-control equipment and the twilight shadows of 19th-century Japan onstage. It is a dark area, crowded with stagehands wearing T-shirts and tool belts, stage assistants holding clipboards and flashlights, and dressers checking singers' costumes before they go out into the light of Act III.

Chorus members arrive dressed in street clothes—their onstage singing is finished. I have a music stand with a light, and a television monitor gives our chorus conductor, Ernest Knell, a full view of the maestro in the pit. Ernest stands on a ladder so that everyone can see him and the penlight he conducts with. He softly calls out alerts as our cue approaches. Then he counts down the last four bars: "Four, three, two, last," and we join the beautiful music, the night of anguish.

Three and a half minutes later, the "Humming Chorus" is over. The chorus breaks—men for their final backstage location, women for the exits. Electricians quickly move away the music stands and television. I retrace my steps to the downstairs hallway and change instruments. Then my viola and I slip back into the pit to play the tragedy through to its end—until the next time.

ACKNOWLEDGMENTS

The Publisher and Editor of *Making a Musical Life* were pleased to work with Tom Heimberg to bring his vision of this book to fruition. We gratefully acknowledge the tireless help and support of Rosalyn and Erica Heimberg, without whom this book could not have appeared in its complete and present form.

We also thank Arnold Steinhardt and Lincoln Mayorga, who generously read first drafts of this book and shared their memories of the musical histories they shared with Tom Heimberg.

For informational details, we have drawn on the wonderful oral history collection of SFPALM (San Francisco Performing Arts Library and Museum). We would like to acknowledge this work: *Thomas Heimberg: Themes and Recollections of a Life in Music*. Thomas Heimberg, with Basya Petnick. Oral history interviews, December 20, 2005–January 17, 2006. LEGACY Oral History Program, San Francisco Performing Arts Library & Museum, 2006.

The majority of the articles in this book first appeared in the issues of *Strings* Magazine, published by String Letter Publishing. For the exceptions, we acknowledge and thank the following sources: "The Mind in Practice," page 3, was edited from the chapter of the same name in *Playing and Teaching the Viola* (American String Teachers Association, 2005); "An Orchestra Is Split," page 81, first appeared in *San Francisco Classical Voice* (www.sfcv.org), September 7, 1999; "The Freeway Philharmonic," page 90, first appeared in *San Francisco Classical Voice,* September 8, 1998; "In Praise of Prompters," page 103, first appeared in *San Francisco Classical Voice,* July 15, 2003; "Remembering Emile Férir," page 106, first appeared in the *Journal of the American Viola Society* (Winter 2001, Vol. 17, No. 3); "Felix Said," page 110, first appeared as the introduction to *Felix Khuner: 1906–1991, A Violinist's Journey from Vienna's Kolisch Quartet to the San Francisco Symphony and Opera Orchestras,* Regional Oral History Office of the Bancroft Library, University of California, Berkeley (www.khuner.com/history/intro.html); "Puccini's Viola of Love," page 126, first appeared in *Animating Opera,* San Francisco Opera 2005–06 Yearbook (2005); courtesy San Francisco Opera Association.

Other Titles from String Letter Publishing's Backstage Books Series

21st-Century Cellists (*Strings* Magazine Editors)
Price: $14.95
128 pages
330754

21st-Century String Quartets (Edith Eisler)
Price: $12.95
128 pages
330530

21st-Century Violinists (*Strings* Magazine Editors)
Price: $12.95
128 pages
69921

A Cellist's Life (Colin Hampton)
Price: $12.95
104 pages
330753

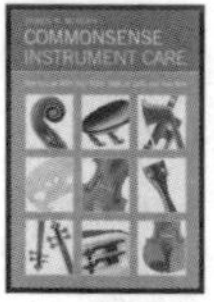

Commonsense Instrument Care (James N. McKean)
Price: $9.95
64 pages
330444

Making Your Living as a String Player (Greg Cahill)
Price: $12.95
96 pages
331094

Violin Owner's Manual (*Strings* Magazine Editors)
Price: $14.95
152 pages
330762

Violin Virtuosos (*Strings* Magazine Editors)
Price: $12.95
128 pages
330566

Try a free issue of *Strings* Magazine!
Call (800) 827-6837 or visit us online at: www.stringsmagazine.com